Why Zarmina Sings

Praise for *Why Zarmina Sings*

I like thinking about this book as a staircase, wherein every new cohort presents a challenge, which forces you to look outside yourself and then inside yourself to select and then master a new skill or strategy. Then you take a step and find another puzzle to work out, but it's only because you've climbed that far can you manage to tackle this new challenge, and so on and so forth. Another element of your story that I appreciate is how you see every class as singular, and you approach teaching each group in their own right. Because I'm wary of anyone telling me "this neat trick will work for everyone," your quiver of methods is very appealing.

—Sara Haxby,
Outdoor and Travel Writer

As someone who holds an MA in Education, it's nice to see a book about education that can be accessed by anyone of any academic level. Thérèse Ayla Kravetz has created a highly readable collection with a personal touch to its narrative, explaining the chemical reactions of the brain in effective terms and without overdoing the amount of information. Her central concept of "re-wiring" the brain by changing techniques of voice, breath, movement, and central concentration forces students to think about themselves in a new way, dispelling anxiety and encouraging them to refocus that anxious energy into something new and productive. *Why Zarmina Sings: 18 Steps to Live and Learn Beyond Anxiety* is an excellent guide for both educators looking to instill confidence, and those who want to improve their own issues of anxiety and self-doubt.

—K.C. Finn, Writer and
Creative Writing Teacher

While I am not currently involved in the teaching profession, I was fascinated by Thérèse Ayla Kravetz' non-fiction educational work, *Why Zarmina Sings: 18 Steps to Live and Learn Beyond Anxiety*. I do have some background in ESL and appreciated her awareness of the cultural differences ESL students bring to the educational table and thought her solutions were creative and inspirational. I was especially intrigued by her use of Shakespeare, Oscar Wilde, and other playwrights' works in the classroom and enjoyed reading about how her students were able to transform themselves through acting.

—Jack Magnus

Anxiety and stress are two strong forces that plague the minds and bodies of many individuals. Learning to cope and live with these negative energies can be very challenging. *Why Zarmina Sings: 18 Steps to Live and Learn Beyond Anxiety* by Thérèse Ayla Kravetz is a helpful resource that can give anxious people, especially students, the tools needed to combat fear, negative thoughts, "what if" scenarios, and worry. It will help them to overcome stage fright and eliminate the fear of oral presentations, while injecting them with more confidence, courage, and inner peace.

—Reader's Favorite 5-Star Review

WHY
Zarmina
SINGS

18 STEPS TO LIVE AND LEARN BEYOND ANXIETY

Thérèse Ayla Kravetz

Why Zarmina Sings
18 Steps to Live and Learn Beyond Anxiety
Copyright © 2016 Thérèse Ayla Kravetz

ISBN: 978-1530468706
LCCN: 2016904360

Design and typesetting: Robin Adams McBride

Printed in U.S.A. by
CreateSpace Independent Publishing Platform,
North Charleston, SC

Thank you Mike Kravetz, for everything.

Table of Contents

Author's Note

This work of nonfiction is a self-help/memoir hybrid based on my experiences in the classroom and life. I have recreated events, locales and conversations to the best of my memory. All the stories are true, though I have changed the names of many individuals and places to protect the privacy of the people involved.

Zarmina's Story

She was always looking for permission. Permission to move. Permission to speak. Permission to be.

She walked on eggshells, sat in the end of the front row by the window, headscarf tightly tied around her neck. She wore a flannel shirt and jeans, and seldom spoke, though always attentive. If she raised her hand, it crimped close to her body and a sweet, soft voice sprang from her.

"Good afternoon," I'd say. A quiet head nod was her only response. Her English was elementary, but she had a gentle smile for me and all her classmates.

Zarmina was a short, sweet Afghan woman, older than most of the students, about forty. It was the spring semester. I was a new professor, teaching college preparatory English to an intermediate reading class. It was the final week of classes and Zarmina's turn to make a presentation for her final grade. I had asked the students to take an historical reference from the book and give an oral presentation on the topic. The rest of the students had given their speeches using the format I'd given them, following the rules of research.

She whispered in a soft, timid voice. "Would it be all right? Would you mind if—"

"Of course," I said. "Please, go next." I grabbed an evaluation rubric from my notebook and got ready to take some notes on her presentation.

She rose, shuffled to the front of the class, and adjusted her scarf. The sides of her face were covered, but her mouth and eyes were bare, and some neat black hair slipped through at the top.

She cleared her voice. "My topic is African American spiritual songs. Would it be all right—?"

She began again, "I mean… would it be okay to sing a short song from a CD I got from the library?"

"Sure," I said. As she stepped to the front of the class, I glanced out the window and saw the last pink reflections of the day's sunlight straddle the horizon.

She turned towards her classmates and out of her mouth trickled "Swing Low, Sweet Chariot." With each line of the spiritual, she eased into the melody. She straightened her body, all five feet of her, and her voice floated out.

"Well, I looked over Jordan and what did I see, comin' for to carry me home…"

Her sound came from far underground, as though it reached to the grounds of Afghanistan and back—to this country's blood, sweat, and tears. As the sound grew in volume, the notes rang through her body, touching all of us, transporting us to another place. At one point, she turned her head to face the window, as if trying to forget the limits of the white-walled, bare classroom and gawking students. Or maybe to travel in her mind.

"Tell all my friends I'm comin' too…," her voice rang sweet and vibrant.

She finished. It took us all a moment to return to the class. Zarmina's eyes sparkled; a brief comfortable smile emerged.

A moment passed and we erupted into clapping. We wiped our wet faces with our fingers and sleeves as she returned to her seat.

I drove home after class in wonder, street lights pointing the way. Zarmina's sound and her luminous performance rang through me. What was it that allowed this shy student to belt out this Negro spiritual and move us to tears? I had given her a broad choice of oral report topics but never mentioned singing. And yet, she recreated the historical moment through song and performance and connected to each of us.

Zarmina's story is my story, too. I circled life's opportunities, wanting to belt out my song, but was too filled with anxiety and introversion to do so. Zarmina's story is my story because like many, I looked for permission to "become" my authentic self. I wanted to break through limitations like anxiety, and free myself from self-criticism and doubt so that I could connect to others.

I wanted to be that kind of teacher, too—the one who helps each student release the song inside of them.

This book is about my own journey from anxiety to expression, along with the stories of my students. I share my own self-doubt, paralyzing fears, how I failed at times, and how I faced myself. I share techniques I learned to help myself and my students, such as qigong, vocal release work, and comedic improvisation to bypass anxiety and accelerate learning.

In over fifteen years in the college classroom, I have seen shy students afraid to speak out in class and angry, solemn students transform into cooperative social students in a matter of weeks because they practiced these tools in class.

My hope is that these stories trigger something in the reader—maybe how to use the imagination more, let go of a fear, move beyond a stammering voice, or take the next step in creativity.

When you teach from fear, study from fear, act from fear, you limit yourself, limit how much you communicate with others, and—according to neuroscience—limit your brain functioning.

Not too long ago, I watched Yo-Yo Ma share his ideas on creativity and success with Charlie Rose: "Listening is most important," he said. "If you are listening and playing, your whole ego is not put into the music, and you are now creating space mentally for others. The skills you need to make music are collaboration, innovation, imagination...these are the same skills you need in the 21st century."[1]

The skills I want to teach my students are reading, writing, and speaking, not just to parrot back information. My hope is that they'll learn to rely on their imaginations to use the information they've learned to create something new, connect with one another, and find the most effective use of their talents in the world.

Learning to be in the moment is the cure for anxiety and more creativity, but we need tools to help us navigate our learning and creativity. In this book, I share stories of the glass ceilings I had to shatter to express myself creatively, and the tools I found or created that helped me to live spontaneously with more joy and freedom.

CHAPTER 1

My Story

*I will face my fear. I will permit it
to pass over me and through me.*
—Frank Herbert, *Dune*[1]

I was twelve when I faced my best friend, Ellen, in a tennis tour-
nament. My mother had been bringing my three brothers and
me to the public courts since I was five to escape chaos in our
alpha-boy house. She was busy: she'd had the four of us within
five years. To help expend some of our extra energy, she and
my father encouraged us to play any sport, including tennis,
baseball, skiing, and basketball.

Ellen had taken up tennis only months before. I had been
competing in tournaments for years. We now stood opposite
each other in a tournament match, while her mother scruti-
nized from the sidelines. With curly symmetrical hair turned
under on each side, skinny capri pants and an L. L. Bean
sweater, her mother looked like Mary Tyler Moore. My mother
avoided the scene.

My mom suffered from moods. Her temper would flare or
she would suddenly disappear to a dark place where she stopped
talking. When I tried to get close at those times, she lashed out. I
learned to retreat to sports or to sit outside under the pine trees,

5

stomach queasy and chest heavy. As a child, I always assumed it was my fault and sought ways to make her happy. I tried to predict her mood or take her side in arguments at home. I was a hypervigilant people-pleaser—I wanted to create peace wherever there was conflict. But that day, I missed her showing up at my matches and my life.

My friend Ellen stood taller than me in the September heat, and wore long black braids evenly knitted on each side. My shorts doubled as basketball practice shorts. My whites were wrinkled, my leather sneakers scuffed, and my hair, long and blonde, had loose wisps that covered my face, blocking vision. Ellen's tennis skirt, shirt and shoes seemed whiter than white, plucked from a sports catalog. As we walked out to the courts, I tried to kick off old dirt from the bottom of my shoes.

This wasn't about the Zen of tennis, or who had more fun. It was about the whole package: clothes, hair, confidence, and attitude. Next to my friend's well-coiffed hair and confident forehands, I felt orphaned and anxious.

Ellen's mom had come to win and dressed herself and her daughter in winning clothes and a winning attitude. This was a competitive tournament match, no longer neighborhood play.

As I walked out on the court that day, my knees shook. Ellen opened a can of balls and we took our separate sides, saying nothing. As I approached the baseline, my breathing sped up.

How could I beat my friend? But how could I lose when I had practiced almost every warm day on the backboard for seven years? The pressure of performance seized my brain so that there was little creativity or flow. A fight or flight reaction kicked in, and, beyond all reason, I felt like it was time to run for my life, die kicking and screaming, or freeze.

I stuffed my feelings, won the toss, and elected to serve, while Ellen chose the shady side. I served into the sun for game one. The tennis ball felt heavy and sticky. I had to push the ball up for the serve, and there were electrical disturbances between my brain and body that blocked my arm from moving at its normal speed or ease.

My backhand had half its power. Instead of confidently stepping into the ball, I leaned back on my heels and the ball dropped short into her side of the court or went into the net. I abandoned rushing the net where I normally had the most fun cutting off the ball early.

At the end of the match, I watched this other Thérèse walk up to the net to shake hands. Ellen had won. I looked up at Ellen's mom and she was beaming— lipstick and hair in place. I had made her day. But I felt betrayed by my own body and mind.

After the match, I stumbled across the street to the town cemetery and sought comfort under the shade of the grandfatherly maple trees. Why had I suddenly lost control of my muscles and my favorite game? I was unaware that "anxious brain" had taken over, destroying my rhythm and muscle coordination, killing my ability to focus on the ball and just be in my body.

I was un-aware that "anxious brain" had taken over, destroying my rhythm and muscle coordi-nation, killing my ability to focus on the ball and just be in my body.

The Anxious Brain

It's no surprise that anxiety can shut down both our minds and our muscles. Even when students want to learn, fear or body tension can make this impossible. My niece, a recent graduate from an arts college, told me about the anxiety she felt. "I had many moments [when] I was afraid to raise my hand just in fear of not being correct," she said, "even though that defeats the purpose of learning."

"Did you have any classes where you felt like yourself?" I asked her one night over the phone.

7

She didn't hesitate. "The acting classes. You're not just a listener there. You are stretching, doing improvisation, constantly using your body.... I was more myself in those classes than anywhere."

This fit with my experience too. Acting had saved me because it gave me permission to be who I really was, and move away from the fight/flight/freeze response. If you are a nontraditional learner with high anxiety, as I was, you rarely get that permission in a traditional classroom. Instead, you are rewarded for remembering visual cues like what's on the blackboard and in the textbook, often in a competitive test situation, and for oral cues when the teacher speaks and you raise your hand to reply. My sense for the dramatic, and my ability to perform aerial flips from the bars on the playground, didn't win me gold stars in the classroom.

Fight or Flight in School

In elementary school, my teacher's voice had power: it could rate me, dismiss me, or bring me joy. If she called on me, I strained to parrot back what I thought she wanted to hear. But when I had to speak, something squeezed my throat—and choked the little bit of sound that trickled out. There was a part of me that wanted to break out, to perform. But I didn't know how and it didn't feel safe.

When the bell rang for recess, though, I knew what to do. I flew out the door and onto the exercise bars and foursquare court. I knew how to build forts, dodge anything my brothers threw at me, and play baseball. I knew to stay down to pick up a ground ball, and run on anything I hit. I had faith in team play and muscle memory.

But in the classroom, I went back into my shell. The shell I lived in for much of my life is described as the fight or flight mechanism. You can also "freeze" in this shell. Neuroscientists use fMRI (functional magnetic resonance imaging) machines to map changes in blood oxygenation and flow that show neural activity; these maps show us which parts of the brain are involved in a particular mental process.[2]

They can see how stress disrupts the higher learning centers. Under certain emotional stresses, the brain cannot process problems, remember details, or make decisions easily. It's often referred to as "lizard brain," because it is leftover from the early evolution of humans when they needed all their energy to fight or flee to save their lives. Robert Sapolsky, professor of neuroscience and neurosurgery at Stanford University, reminds us that "Stress can interfere with learning, and it can be very difficult to turn this around."[3]

"Stress can interfere with learning, and it can be very difficult to turn this around."[3]

Different Learning Styles

"You don't have vhaat it takes to learn German!" my stout German professor with a sharp nose and a thick accent told me after midterm exams. It was already my sophomore year in college when she gave me my progress report. German was my declared major, and I had been studying it for three semesters.

I sat in my chair and gulped down the pain of this remark. I found no words to respond. She just held out my midterm, which had a D, and moved on to another student.

I wandered back to my dorm room and sat down on my bed. I was performing miserably. Thoughts raced through my mind: What would I tell my parents who were paying for this education? How did I get into this competitive school? Somebody in admissions must have let my application slip through.

9

I would later figure out that the competitive classroom, which contradicted my kinesthetic learning style (the need to move and engage the body in order to learn), and my own anxiety about how I measured up with the other students, inhibited me from learning the language.

I decided to give it one last try before admitting failure to my parents and myself. I could go to Germany, immerse myself. What did I have to lose? The grass certainly looked greener in Germany than at my college. I filled out the application to study abroad the next semester and within months, I was on a plane to Tübingen.

The day after I moved into my dorm room in Germany, I walked into the small community kitchen on the 7th floor. The dim lights illuminated bare but clean counters. I had brought my strainer, milk, and coffee from my room, rather than stake a claim in the communal cabinets. The only two students present, Helmut and Valerie, were the most patient with the new "Ammies" who came over each semester and developed an over-fondness for quality beer (as evidenced by stacks of empty cases in the hallways).

That morning my new German dorm mates greeted me with gentle smiles, then guided me through codes of dorm behavior. To fill in where my German vocabulary could not, they used exaggerated physical gestures. They stayed away from the local Schwäbisch dialect, and offered simple questions in High German such as, "Woher kommst du?" (Where are you from?), "Wie lange bleibst du hier?" (How long are you staying for?), and "Möchtest du einen kaffee trinken?" (Coffee?).

After that day, we frequently gathered in the kitchen to make a group meal. I learned how to make spätzle, and boil it till it floated to the top, indicating it was done. My new friends gave me words for each step of meal preparation and cleanup, as we exchanged trust, friendship, language, and Weissbier.

Later I signed up for the local basketball team. I ran up and down the court while the coach called out commands, "auszeit" (timeout) and "werfen sie den ball" (throw it), while I hollered at my teammates "hier" and "frei." These movement moments formed solid learning for the new language in my body and brain. Fluency grew out of this kinesthetic experience, my natural style. I had moments of safety, necessity, and play in the kitchen and on the court. I didn't have a stoic teacher staring down at me, but instead a friendly face who needed something I could deliver.

I remember the moment, one month later when, yawning and strolling down the hallway, I walked into the kitchen and grabbed my coffee and strainer from my section of the cupboards. As I put my coffee down on the free spot on the table, I said without thinking, "Wie geht es dir heute morgen?" (How are you doing this morning?). I heard these words as they came out of me so effortlessly, like a river rolling easily over rocks.

Helmut and Valerie answered "gut," unaware of the linguistic mountain I had climbed a second ago. I eased into my chair, eager to try to catch the conversation as it flowed back and forth in my new language.

There were subtler changes happening to me as I learned German that year. I remember walking over a small bridge to a shop later that week in the light drops of rain. I grabbed the shopping cart and roamed through aisles of well-organized cheeses and breads to the counter. As I ordered the knockwurst, kraut, and brotchen, I could *feel* the words coming out of me, grounding me, as I spoke. Many words contained consonants and guttural sounds instead of vowels. I could no longer hide behind the

11

I had a new sound. I was a new sound.

breathy, soft voice, which defined my native English voice. I had to speak in a new way.

It was as if more of me was suddenly released into the world. I had a new sound. I was a new sound.

I returned to college for my senior year after living in Germany for nine months, and got As in German for the first time—a big step up from barely making Cs and Ds the previous year.

Voice and Identity

Our voices reveal our stories. Who was I if I wasn't the only girl in the family, a Bostonian or raised in a religious family? I didn't even know I had a breathy voice until I moved to Germany and had to make guttural sounds, which required more air. My voice revealed this to me.

How we actually speak a language also reveals our identity. "We grew up with many siblings and we speak loud in public" or "We are from Vietnam, so we speak this way to our elders," or "Men from our family speak this way." We are the words we speak, the voice we use.

Often we don't know what we identify with until we try to change. That's the beauty of learning in an environment that fits our learning style. When I tried to speak German in Germany where there was no choice, I had to let go of this tendency to put breath behind my sound instead of resonance. I had to stop swallowing the ends of sentences. In German, when you open your mouth, you end the sentence with the verb. This makes it necessary to line up all your details and prepositional phrases early. German is not approximate. The many consonant sounds force you to commit to the breaks in your vowel sounds. It has a neuter, masculine, and feminine case, so there is also precision using nouns.

The bakeries, the cafès, my friends, the bus driver, were a natural part of my everyday surroundings. I had to eat, travel, socialize. So I dropped the fears and anxieties, which had always blocked my ability to learn, to remember, and to speak. This was my life, not just my classroom. I felt safe to experiment in front of friends who weren't grading me.

As I played basketball, I also put the language in my body. I learned from the coach who gave me feedback and from listening to teammates. Collaborating with teammates got me out of that fight or flight brain state that I suffered from. I didn't feel stuck in my emotional brain firing its stress hormones because positive emotions and friendships were letting me open to learning both the culture and the language.

"the adult brain retains impressive powers of 'neuroplasticity'—the ability to change its structure and function in response to experience."[4]

It's all brain science. And these are exciting times. In *TIME*'s online article, "The Brain: How the Brain Rewires Itself," Sharon Begley tells us that "the adult brain retains impressive powers of 'neuroplasticity'—the ability to change its structure and function in response to experience."[4] But I learned, in Germany and at home, that this ability to change requires learning activities that are outside the box, learning that uses more of the whole person.

Going to Germany was like putting on a costume or trying on a new role. I was creating new synapses, new pathways of learning, to rewire my brain. And something else happened when I spoke German. There was more of me in the room.

I liked this transformation, and I found more of it with voice work.

CHAPTER 2

Free Your Voice!

The human voice is the expression of the self.... Our voices express
us in profound ways, and reveal our selves, our lives, our hearts, our
souls, and our journeys through life.
—Alfred Wolfsohn[1]

Learning German began to expand my sound. But I still de-
faulted to a breathy voice, and lacked confidence to speak freely.
I wonder now if my weekly trips to the chiropractor for jaw
and neck pain were related to hiding my thoughts and swallowing my vocal sound.

Around this time I enrolled at Lesley University in Cambridge, Massachusetts to get a master's degree in expressive
therapies. I had taken one of those career personality tests and
"dance therapist" came up as the number one career for me.
The combination of the arts and therapy spoke to me, so I
thought I would dip my toes in. One of the classes was called
"voice for actors," and my teacher was a South African actress
who had studied with students of Roy Hart, from the lineage
of voice coach Alfred Wolfsohn.

In her voice classes, we started by grounding ourselves. We
rolled from one end of the room to the other on the wood
floor, like kids rolling down the side of a hill. My teacher would
say as we rolled: "You are 80 percent liquid, so feeeeeel it," in

15

her elegant Afrikaans accent. The rolling melted the tension in my body and my mind.

Then we imagined wearing heavy space boots and trudged around the room in slow motion. The slow motion slowed my mind and emotions to where they were in sync with my breath.

Next, we let go of tension by rolling up the spine, vertebrae by vertebrae, and vocalizing by "allowing the sound to emerge." The sound that emerged was unforced, deep, and natural, not loud. The goal was to connect the breath deep into our bellies and our bodies so that the voice could emerge organically. If you arrive at that connected sound spontaneously as an actor, the audience feels it and believes it. It's authentic, not forced.

If you arrive at that connected sound spontaneously as an actor, the audience feels it and believes it.

During one of these classes, I was standing at the piano with my teacher doing the usual jaw release exercise (see exercise box, page 22) as she played different notes up and down the scale. I had been working with her for about six weeks on voice release work, and she often had us standing by the piano while we were sounding out.

I had some neck pain, and we were releasing some sound as I gently pulled down on the lower jaw with my hands to get the jaw to release. Then I took my hands off my jaw and just allowed my whole mouth to open wide with a loud "aaaahhh" and "oooohhh" as she moved down the scale of the piano, and I followed with my voice.

I felt a shift. My mouth opened wider and muscles relaxed in my neck. The teacher stood up and gently put a hand on my neck as a loud clear sound that I had never heard before bellowed out. It was wide, rich, untamed. It broke down a wall of resistance. I felt a burden lift that I hadn't known

16

I was carrying. The sound vibration eased the tension in my neck.

Tears fell as emotions and old tightness released. My teacher smiled to encourage me to continue. I let my neck stretch to the side as I let more of the sound out. I giggled and felt as if some old crusty behavior had been removed and I was free to communicate with strength and ease.

I returned my focus to the room and noticed my neck pain was almost gone. My jaw was no longer locked in a half-open frozen position, but wide open. It felt like every sound behind each word I'd hidden from the world blew out of me. I had felt a shift learning German, but this vocal experience showed me a voice that was strong, deep, and linked to a part of me, a voice I hadn't acknowledged before.

I was getting curious now—the craft of vocal release and this type of theater wasn't about being the best or sounding pretty, but about releasing tension, and being authentic. I took more workshops with voice teachers and studied the vocal work of Kristin Linklater, a famous British coach who had developed a more linear method of releasing the voice for actors. But I was drawn especially to those students who had trained in France with the Roy Hart Theatre, in the lineage of Alfred Wolfsohn.

Alfred Wolfsohn

Roy Hart developed a theater in the 1960s after the death of his teacher Alfred Wolfsohn, who was born in 1896 in Berlin. At eighteen, Wolfsohn was drafted into the army in World War I. He was severely wounded and by the end of the war was diagnosed with shell shock, or what we'd now call post-traumatic stress disorder.

In 1919, he was finally discharged from a German military hospital, but was still suffering from mustard gas poisoning and combat trauma. The doctors could give him no further treatment.

A singer before the war, his voice suffered too.

In the trenches, Wolfsohn had heard the terrible cries of injured and dying men. After the war, he suffered from aural hallucinations where he kept hearing those sounds of agony over and over again in his mind. When he started to try to sing himself, he couldn't produce the sounds he knew he was capable of. He studied with voice teachers, but none could repair the damage that had been done to his voice just from living through those horrific experiences during the war. So he began a study of psychology, including the work of Carl Jung. As he tried to free himself of the voices of dying soldiers in his head and repair his own voice, he saw a connection between the psyche and the voice.

Wolfsohn began to give singing lessons. He found that most issues were not caused by a larynx malfunction, but by emotional and mental stress that could be repaired. He was able to provide emotional and psychic relief through vocal release with his students. One of his students noticed that "he gained an immediate insight into a person's character from their voice, listening to the vibrations of their inner world."[2]

This same student shared how Wolfsohn taught: "Lessons lasted about forty-five minutes...and until 1958 were always one-to-one: You were just asked to sing a note. Following this, his directions depended upon his perception of that sound, the need to open it more, make it louder, form it more freely, centre it more in the head or more in the stomach.... There was no recipe, no technique, only a deep and close understanding of the pupil standing before him."[3]

From Cambridge to New York City

Soon after my voice classes with teachers from Wolfsohn's lineage, I interrupted my degree program and moved to New York City. The discoveries I'd made through voice and theater fed me and freed me. I wanted to be an actor. I wanted more.

18

In New York, I took courses in voice and acting, studying with Catherine Fitzmaurice, an American voice coach. I continued to study the work of Kristin Linklater, the British vocal coach. I taught part-time and took course work in education.

I began traveling to perform. I was working on a play in Virginia one summer and began to help some of the actors increase their volume and resonance using these vocal exercises. It was in this time period that I began teaching workshops at a local actors' resource center. When I noticed tension in others' voices, I'd create an exercise or use one I had learned to release it. For example, a nasal voice told me I needed to help the person resonate more in the chest area. It was creative, fun, and exhilarating.

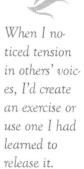

When I noticed tension in others' voices, I'd create an exercise or use one I had learned to release it.

I remember one student, Karen, who came to me for voice lessons. We went through some warm-ups in the studio space I had rented. Then I went to my keyboard to play some simple notes starting at middle C. She sang out on "aaaahhh" and slowly moved up the scale. I noticed she stood straight but locked her knees as she sang. I went over and gently put my hands behind her knees.

"Now, just sound out on that same note, Karen" and she began.

With softly bent knees, the sound "aaaahhh" popped out of her in a new way. Ah-ha, I thought. More proof of the voice-body link.

Sometimes in class I would gently shake an arm as the student was sounding out or make some other slight contact. Other times I showed students how to engage more of their belly in the sound by bending and vocalizing. I could tell if there was restriction that was blocking

19

their breath and voice, and what to do about it.

Information about this came through a sensing and intuition that was unsettling to me at the time. My mind wanted specific steps to guide me, proof that I was doing the right thing. All I had was a toolkit full of vocal release exercises on which to rely in the spur of the moment. But the process was not linear, and it took time to trust it.

In one session in my studio, after a typical warm-up of stretching, breathing, shoulder shrugs, and sounding out, I practiced some relaxation exercises with a student at the piano. As I played each note and she sang up the scales to the higher registers, she discovered a huge upper register that she hadn't used before. She was opening up with new sound, singing high-pitched perfect tones towards the end of the keys on the piano. I was almost at the end of my keyboard and her sound was still beautiful and buttery.

Suddenly she choked up and started to cry. I stopped playing and looked up at her. "Are you all right?"

"I just dropped right back to when I was three years old," she said.

"What happened then?"

"I was in an accident, and my tongue was cut open. It was bleeding profusely. And I went right back there." She had discovered an upper register of sound that had shut down when she'd had the accident. She had released something that was stuck back in time. Now she was beaming, loving her own voice. Just from a simple vocal exercise.

We finished our lesson as the late morning sunlight lit up the wooden floors of the studio.

In one vocal exercise I got from voice coach Richard Armstrong (from the Roy Hart Theatre troupe), I taught my students to role-play and move as an elf, a duchess, or a giant as they made sounds. As they embodied these personas, they played with putting the voice into very different parts of the body. The duchess had resonance in her chest, and I can remember the joy and freedom walking around the wooden floor of the classroom talking like a duchess: "You may go now" and "I would like some tea." My chest even stuck out slightly so I could feel the resonance there. The elf was the nasal voice. When we acted like elves, we hunched over and sometimes had our hands by the sides of our heads to remind us to "put the sound in our nasal cavities." For the sound of the giant, we moved slower and stood with bent knees and a wide stance. We tried to connect to sound in the belly.

Another exercise I learned from the Roy Hart teachers was to open the throat so that our voices resembled the words we sung out. For example, I could sing the word "flute" with a small width of the throat, and open it up a little bit more to sing the word "clarinet," and then completely wide for "saxophone." Each time I sang a different word, the feel of the sound changed. Actors loved this vocal flexibility, as it was a key in helping them explore their characters.

When I worked with trained singers, I told them, "Let go of everything you've learned. Instead, we're going to discover a new sound and we're going to play with your range. Then you can add the technique back in." The result was a greater vocal range, sometimes even an octave in one or two sessions.

One opera singer, a tenor, was frustrated with his weak lower register. We did various warm-ups with the breath. I directed my exercises to engage his belly instead of his head and chest voice. I asked him to bend down and pick up an imaginary ball off the floor as

Let go of everything you've learned. Instead, we're going to discover a new sound. . . .

21

he sang out different sounds for prolonged periods. As he went down to the floor I asked him to imagine the lowest note he could and sound it out. I did the motion and sound with him.

"I don't want pretty," I stressed. "Just let the sound emerge."

In two sessions, he found a new depth in his voice.

The Jaw: Gateway to Sound

I named the jaw the "Gateway to Sound" because if you're afraid to talk, the jaw will close and tighten up, and can affect both pronunciation and the depth of vocal resonance. The jaw exercise comes from Kristin Linklater's work, and it was a breakthrough for me.[4]

Make a loose fist and hold your lower jaw gently with the knuckles of each hand. Point your fingertips towards the floor while your knuckles are holding the lower jaw, and thumb is below the chin. Palms are towards your face. With your head level (without arching your neck) gently pull down the lower jaw and with your bent fingers still on it, let it release to close. The upper jaw doesn't move.

You will probably notice some resistance when you try to pull it down. Be sure to add some sound as you are gently pulling and releasing the jaw. The sound helps release tension. The sound can be "aaaahhh." Push down and let the jaw come up many times while sounding out "aaaahhh." After a few sessions, there will be a difference in tension and sound.

One of my voice coaches, Catherine Fitzmaurice, said, "All of this is about listening, actually. Even the feeling into your own vibration is about listening in to yourself. As you become more capable of feeling your own vibration, you become capable of feeling other actors' vibrations."[5]

"All of this is about listening, actually...."[5]

Wolfsohn's Method: Be in the Moment with the Student

I began to trust my intuition, but after entering higher education, was again confronted with the tension between the creative brain and the rational brain. In this world of results-oriented testing like the SAT and ACT, operating in the here and now with a method that emerges from the students who are in front of you can be daunting.

But this voice work—teaching and studying it—was a crucial step in my journey to rewire my anxious brain and body. I knew that. I set about expanding my repertoire of nontraditional teaching tools.

I was greatly reassured when I read how Alfred Wolfsohn's students described his teaching: "He had no method," one of them said. "His only method was to listen and observe, then depending upon what he heard, he would take the next step.... Every lesson was adapted for each pupil and...related to the human being and his voice in the here and now."[6] He was quite successful. Recordings of his students, like Roy Hart who had eight octave ranges, can still be heard at Smithsonian Folkways.[7]

My winding career path had given me tools to combine voice work, acting, movement, and teaching, but I was creating my own "method" for language learning, pronunciation, and vocal release for students.

Emilia from Colombia spoke with a very nasal voice. She didn't open her mouth enough to pronounce sounds like "oh" and "ah." It was very difficult to understand her pronunciation and she knew it. A petite figure dressed in tailored shirts and pants with long black hair, she rarely spoke.

She came to me one afternoon after class, her eyes pleading and sad, squeezing her words out: "I really have problems with people understanding me."

I could see the stiffness in her jaw. I could see she had trouble moving her tongue into positions for American English. When she spoke, most of the sound was directed up through the sinuses.

We had some time before the next class came in, so I suggested we work on her poem.

She pulled out Emily Dickinson's "Because I Could Not Stop for Death" and began to read. I stopped her.

"Let's try something, Emilia. Let's do an exercise to loosen that jaw tension. I can see that you hold a lot of it there. Did you ever notice that?"

"People always ask me to repeat everything," she said, nodding. I could tell it frustrated her.

We stood up and did a yawn/sigh exercise twice: a big yawn with some sound. It helps to engage your whole body and arms in the yawn before you release a sigh.

The first time, Emilia only opened her mouth half way. Shy by nature, it was hard to get her to do the opposite of her habitual tight jaw, but she smiled and tried it.

"I can feel the tightness in the jaw now," she said. "But it's more open."

Then I asked her to blow through her lips to let go of

tightness; she was holding a lot of tension there, too, and it impeded her pronunciation. Then I stuck out my tongue and told her to do the same (we needed to stretch this very tight muscle). She giggled but went ahead with it.

We returned to the poem, and she went through a stanza. Her mouth opened a little bit wider now, and I could hear a more resonant, clear voice. There was still a lot of nasal voice in spots but also a hint of the hidden potential.

"Do you feel that difference?" I asked her.

"I don't know why, but I feel a lot of vibration here." She pointed to her nasal sinuses and then averted her eyes to the desk. "I'm louder now." I could see she wanted to shift to this sound even more, but it made her uneasy.

Students need to be reminded that change in pronunciation happens with change in their physical bodies and vocal apparatus; the thought or desire to change has to come with the physical change. It's a common reaction for them to be uncomfortable, hearing themselves in a new way. I could remember how being louder and guttural was a stretch for me when learning German. I sensed not to push Emilia any further at this point.

"I want you to practice this exercise of moving your jaw, the yawn/sigh. And it will help to open the mouth a little wider if you can."

"Thank you," she said, smiled and left.

We did more vocal relaxation exercises in class over the next couple of weeks.

At her poetry reading, she was the first to volunteer. We all waited quietly with our full attention. Emilia opened her mouth a little bit wider than usual and began her poem, her voice less nasal, more resonant. Yes, she still had work to do, but in just a few lessons she had begun to break through the patterns formed over many years.

25

The Calling Exercise

A favorite exercise of mine is the calling exercise. I do this before rehearsals or student presentations when students are nervous and may not be getting enough resonance because of the tightness in their chests or jaw or posture. They may have lost that connection between voice and breath. I usually do this in small groups.

To begin, stand sideways and put your arm out in front of your chest (palm facing your own chest) as if you're about to hit a backhand stroke in tennis. Imagine you're turning to call out to a person in a parking lot across the street.

As you call out: "heeeeyyy!," draw out the vowel sound so it's prolonged, leave your back foot where it is, but move the rest of your body a quarter turn toward the imaginary parking lot. Swing your arm outward as you vocalize, opening your chest (like you are hitting a backhand). Take a short step with your front foot toward the parking lot). Open your hips while moving your whole torso and an arm toward the imaginary person in the parking lot while sounding out.

To repeat the exercise, reverse sides.

The other students nodded as they clapped for her performance. She returned to her chair, sat back down, and let out a sigh.

As I learned to relax the muscles in the mouth, throat, diaphragm, tongue, and rib cage, I learned I could produce new sounds and connect to the essence of words. This affected the way I spoke and how I taught vocal release to actors, but also how I taught English to students for whom it's a second language. Meaning and emotion could be captured in the sounds of many words—especially the older words.

In general, vowels allow for emotion to emerge while consonants generate the meaning of words through the phonetic barriers of teeth, lips, and tongue. Enunciating a word using its consonants gives it boundaries and meaning. When I make the sound "aaaahhh" for a prolonged period I feel an easy joy. When I make another vowel sound like "eeeehhh" I feel excitement or nervousness. (If you're stiff, you won't be able to feel the words. You have to have the openness and relaxation to let the word pronounce itself through you.)

In general, vowels allow for emotion to emerge while consonants generate the meaning of words through the phonetic barriers of teeth, lips, and tongue.

Emotional Vowels

Try to make one of these vowel sounds now, and see if you can hear or feel some kind of emotion releasing as you say it. Try opening your mouth wide with an "aaaahhh." After a few moments, you'll feel some relief. And "eeeehhh" brings a different sort of feeling, as does "oooohhh."

Older English or French words, such as those in plays by Shakespeare and Moliere, are formed out of the experience itself. For example, suppose you never knew what the word *bubble* meant. If your lips are relaxed, and you allow your cheeks to fill up with air, and you say the word *bubble*, you are a bubble. A lot of the old English words imitate or suggest what they describe, a phenomenon known as onomatopoeia.

27

Take the word *splat*. It sounds like something landing with a squish. If you relax your mouth and jaw more than you normally do and say the following words, you can get a sense of the kinesthetic feeling words can give you as you say them. *Boom*, *crack*, and *tap-tap-tap* are clear examples.

But I can hear some of the emotion and meaning in words like *weary* or *rude*, *beautiful* or *violence*, if I give time to the vowels and have clear pronunciation of the consonants.

I did the calling exercise (see exercise on page 26) in one Friday night class. Most of the twenty-five students had worked all week, cared for children, and were using the last of their energy to make it up the stairs to room 330. They dropped their heavy bags next to their chairs and slumped into their seats. I smiled and asked them to stand. They slowly forced their bodies up.

The room on this particular night was filled with many students from different countries in Africa; a few were from cultures where women only talk softly in the company of men. Other students came from Latin America and Russia and varied greatly in comfort level and fluency.

I divided them into groups of five or six. I told them to imagine calling to someone out in the parking lot and I pointed out the window to the area of cars fifty yards away. I corralled the first group and made the calling sound with them, moving hands and bodies. They gave me a great loud call; then, surprised at their own sounds, they giggled. Their eyes and bodies were now awake and instead of sitting down again, they stood waiting to hear the next group.

The next group moved slowly into position, turned their bodies and outstretched arms, and made a great loud call. We did the rounds of calling for each group and then returned to our seats. I looked at the students—now smiling, energetic, and sitting upright in their chairs. What had happened?

Using such exercises allowed the students to claim their vocal power and sidestep cultural and personal limitations they may have had about their own voice for a long time. And as I witnessed, this can happen in just a few minutes.

When some students from my oral communication class stopped by to join me in the cafeteria one spring afternoon, they told me my class had helped them. I asked how.

Ayshe, from Turkey, leaned forward in her chair with an energy behind her eyes. "When we come to class," she said, "we are speaking with our whole body and the brain is awake to accept the information." So simple: wake up the body and the voice so the brain can function.

Relaxing the tongue and jaw, and connecting to the breath with your voice, can help you shake off patterns of physical tension, but it can affect emotions, too. If you are shy or anxious, it can help you speak out more or balance your nervousness.

Education in the 21st century needs to be a path to greater self-awareness. Our emotions, our bodies, our voices are not separate from our minds. Each helps the other function more effectively. When we have experiences in more of the senses, more of the voice and the body, we remember more, we assimilate more, and we communicate more.

But this experimentation, this change, this new way of operating in the world, can feel like a risk. What do we do about that?

Using such exercises allowed the students to claim their vocal power and sidestep cultural and personal limitations

CHAPTER 3

Follow Your Passion or ...

Woody Allen started out as a comedy writer. At age nineteen, his managers told him he was also an entertainer, but Allen saw himself more of a writer, maybe because of his terrible stage fright. Nevertheless, he agreed to try stage work for a year. For a year, Allen performed for a live audience and failed repeatedly. He was interesting and unique, but the crowd didn't get his humor. Then something changed.

Allen started to think about what was funny to *him*, what jokes made him laugh instead of trying to predict what would make the audience laugh. He was now in what Julian Ford and Jon Wortmann refer to as "learning brain." The stage fright was still there, but his anxiety took a back seat to the learning brain in order to do what he was interested in. The audience loved it. Many greats suffered from stage fright, write Ford and Wortmann. Lawrence Olivier had to be pushed on stage. Barbra Streisand, forgetting a lyric in Central Park one day in 1967, didn't return to the stage for thirty years.[1]

I often had stage fright too. When I taught or acted, I panicked. In front of students, this panic interfered with my

31

effectiveness as a teacher. So I eventually learned to rewire and calm my brain with many tools.

One tool came to me unexpectedly after a student's bad review of my class.

"Change the Teacher"

I sat at my classroom desk, the sun peeking through my window. Its light lit up the dust afloat in the air. Leaves from my desk plant, now brown, cried for water. It was close to sundown in late December. The semester had come to a close, and I was reading student comments.

The first two reviews were lukewarm. They dissected my book choice and classroom discussions. Next came a couple of generally positive reviews for both teacher and class. I relaxed a little and began scanning through more of them until I got to one that was blank except for the answer to one question. The question was, "What would you change about this class?" The answer written below was "the teacher."

I dropped the evaluation onto my desk. A tightness grew in my chest until it felt like a knife lodged in there. Unable to sit alone with my thoughts or withering plant, I walked across the hall to spill my worries to a trusted colleague.

"Everyone has a student like that now and then," she assured me.

"I guess so..." I bowed my head to dodge small talk with other teachers who passed by.

"It's not you, Thérèse. Trust me." She put her hand on my shoulder.

I thanked her and wobbled back to my desk, unconvinced. I looked out at the trees whose branches, without their leaves, looked like skeletons. This is all wrong, I thought.

I had agreed to teach a hybrid ESL (English as a Second

Language) class because of a push from the administration. A hybrid class meets partially in person and partially online. Its success depends on the teacher presenting material in a friendly, usable way online so students can keep learning on the days they don't meet in the physical classroom.

But I had been unsure how to transfer the in-class material to the online portion. My brain froze up whenever I went to create curriculum for the online class. I no longer had the cues of an in-person setting, the facial expressions and nonverbal input. How would I know if they were learning? My anxiety created a mental fog. The attitude of some teachers was not helpful, and the lack of honest dialogue triggered more stress. Then I betrayed my instincts again when I chose the same novel as the rest of the teachers for class, even though I felt no connection to the writing, characters, or themes.

It all showed in these evaluations.

The holidays came and went, and I began another semester.

As I walked in to greet my new students in my speaking and listening class, I brought only the textbook. I was reluctantly ready to follow the departmental curriculum to a T. But three weeks into the semester, I started to dislike going to class. This began rubbing off on my students. Amira, a dedicated student under any circumstances, began to fidget in her chair, and others, like Stephanie, arrived five, then ten minutes late. The Sudanese man, Ameen, emailed me to say he could no longer come. The class was drying up.

One day as I sat at my desk trying to prepare, I remembered the evaluation from the last semester that still gave me a cold chill. I saw the line of text from the student: "Change the teacher." Playing it safe last semester had gotten me nowhere.

I can do better! I thought. With my feet up on my desk, I scanned the bookshelf in front of me. My favorite collection of plays caught my eye.

As I leafed through scenes of plays by authors I loved—Oscar Wilde, Henrik Ibsen, Craig Pospisil, Tennesee Williams, Susan Glaspell, Marsha Norman—I thought: What did I have to lose? I loved these stories and I loved theater. Couldn't my students learn using this material instead of our boring textbook?

But I didn't know if I could even direct a scene, much less get students to perform.

. . . the stress of not changing was greater than the fear of change.

At the end of my internal debate, the stress of not changing was greater than the fear of change. I grabbed two one-act plays and five scenes from other well-known plays and flew up the stairs to class. I told them we were going to do something different.

Blank stares met me.

My enthusiasm had gotten ahead of me. "I'd like you to read some scripts I have from plays," I said. "We're going to use these throughout the semester." I walked around and handed out scripts to each student.

At first, my students gripped their scripts and read haltingly. But soon they began to smile at the stories as they heard their voices in class for the first time. Then one student, Terri, glared at me, eyes wide. "Are we going to have to memorize this?" Her sharp rise in tone indicated her anxiety.

"We're going to read these scripts this week," I said. "Each of you will write down on a piece of paper, for me, two or three roles you'd like to play. I'll give you a role to practice for a few weeks with your group. I'll help you get to know your character, what he wants and why he wants it. It's not about performing, it's about listening."

By the following week, I was ready to invite a group of students to read in front of the class. First, I tried to create safety: "Read it slowly," I told them, "take your time, just have fun. I'm here to help." But when I asked for volunteers? Silence. Nothing.

I went to the board and wrote two columns: Risks and Benefits. (These two lists were the same ones I had created in my brain the previous week, before choosing this activity.) We brainstormed. What was the worst thing that could happen if you performed? We went over the gory details of passing out, getting sick, turning red, stumbling, and having people laugh at you. Then we brainstormed benefits of practicing a new language in front of an audience: improved confidence, strengthened communication, better grades and a better future, and speaking up for ourselves.

What was the worst thing that could happen if you performed?

Slowly my students began to change their minds. I helped them connect to their values of learning and their goals for success. We all began to move into "learning brain," the place where we find our natural strengths.

Finally, two students volunteered to play the mother and daughter in the same scene from *'night, Mother* by Marsha Norman. The daughter has planned her suicide, and her mother is in denial of her plan.

The first student, Stephanie, was a twenty-eight-year-old woman from Peru. She had trouble making it to class on time, was aloof and doing poorly on tests, and worked two jobs to support her family back in Peru. Amira, twenty-six, from Iraq, wanted to be a doctor. Two students, so divergent in religion, culture, language, and histories, were now the mother and daughter.

They read the parts out loud slowly in front of the class, peering up at me for encouragement after each line. "Excellent," I said, looking down at the scripts.

I had an idea. "Now, let's hear what it sounds like if you switch roles."

Amira shrugged her shoulders and took the daughter's part and Stephanie took the role of the mother. They began to read again.

"Ricky will grow out of this, Jess, and be a real fine boy" said Stephanie. "But I have to tell you. I wouldn't want Ricky to know we had a gun in the house."

"Here it is, I found it!" piped Amira.

The role reversal had worked! I could see Stephanie's mothering instincts and Amira's assertiveness for the role of the desperate daughter both kick into place.

By the final performance in week ten, Stephanie had managed to work her two jobs, juggle a new relationship, and come to class on time. Amira, too, was ready for the final performance and handed over the script to me, confident she had it memorized. They brought bags of clothing they had picked out for their costumes and ran to the restroom to put them on.

When they returned, Stephanie wore a housecoat and slippers, her hair up in a bun. Amira wore jeans, sneakers, and t-shirt. They approached the front of the class and placed the toy gun they would need in this scene in a desk drawer. The rest of the class watched quietly, looking at me to see my reaction, then back at the actors.

Stephanie lifted her arms to fold her laundry. The tension began to build as the mother denied what the daughter was telling her. "It's just something Ricky's going through. Maybe he's in with some bad people. He just needs some time, sugar." Stephanie's voice and body were shaky but she threw her lines into the audience. Amira gave her cynical response.

"I hope they put him away sometime. I'd turn him in myself if I knew where he was."

Amira's character continued to try to convince her mother that her boy was in trouble and it was her own fault. The mother, Stephanie, denied it again.

The ending of this short scene came to a climax when Stephanie—wanting to hold on to her denial that her daughter will kill herself—erupted in frustration, "Stop that!" I was jolted in my chair and looked at the other students, who also sat up at Stephanie's thunderous response.

Stephanie, this soft-spoken Peruvian woman, had gone where the script asked her to go—into a burst of anger—though it was a cultural taboo to show her anger, a risk to her own self-image.

We all clapped. The two women smiled at each other. They had taken risks and learned to trust themselves, each other, and the masterful playwright who gave the actors good reason to emote.

To try on different hats and perform in front of others is a risk for both teacher and student. But with great scripts, like those I'd pulled off my bookshelf that day, acting out a story is easier. The structure of the scripts, my students' dedication, and the joy of becoming immersed in "learning brain" changed both them and me. Change the teacher, indeed.

Julian Ford and Jon Wortmann discuss many solutions to high anxiety and PTSD in their book, *Hijacked by Your Brain*. In their thirty years of experience, the authors found that focusing on what is important can alleviate the fight, flight, or freeze response.[2] Here I had finally aligned my teaching with my core values of creative expression and storytelling. I was no longer so uptight about what my students were doing every moment of class. I began to relax during our classes, the rehearsals, and performances out of sheer enjoyment.

The students from Amira and Stephanie's class were also more committed to class after I added the drama. They came to class early to chat with me and each other. And though they still had anxiety around performing, each took more risks in speaking up during regular classroom discussions. I took more risks too, adding improvisation, movement, and breath work to each semester's curriculum.

"The problem with stress is that most of us don't know how to turn our brains' alarms down when it is stuck in the 'on' position," Ford and Wortmann explain.[3] Moving into "learning brain" can help—a lot.

Skaters Michelle Kwan and Sarah Hughes starred in the 2002 Olympics. I remember watching Sarah Hughes on TV; I was in awe of her final skate. Kwan was the favorite, but on the night of long skate, Hughes made a change that was visible to me. She said later, "I skated for pure enjoyment. That's how I wanted my Olympic moment to be." I remember thinking Hughes seemed to skate as if in a dream. She smiled in the middle of the performance as she landed on her second triple jump. I realized she had beaten her brain's alarm and anxiety, focusing instead on her love of the sport.

"When you think about your core values, you optimize the partnership between the alarm and the learning brain...."[4]

When your brain gets in the habit of firing alarms from a current or past trauma, it is difficult to think clearly and creatively, Ford and Wortmann write. On the other hand, the thinking brain is happy when in learning mode and can work together with the emotional brain. "When you think about your core values, you optimize the partnership between the alarm and the learning brain. Instead of recalling thoughts that cause alarm emotions like anxiety and fear, under stress your brain recalls what you value most: thoughts that keep you focused on the experiences you enjoy."[4]

In a play, in front of a live audience, we're in learning mode. Anything can happen. Students who were unruly in my class became interested. Students who were bored became motivated. Students who were shy became confident. All because they were suddenly in learning mode.

That first experience using drama became the launching pad for a big shift in my teaching. It also began to rewire my own emotions in the classroom.

Chapter 4

Break Free with Movement

Anh was a twenty-five-year-old Vietnamese student in my oral communication class. Head down, with long, straight, jet-black hair, she spoke in stops and starts. In her culture, it was a custom that she lower her eyes when speaking to elders or people in authority. She also believed it was impolite for her to speak in a loud tone in a classroom situation.

When we began our play that week, she chose the role of Lady Bracknell in a scene I rely on a lot in my classes from *The Importance of Being Earnest*, by Oscar Wilde.

Lady Bracknell is a stodgy aristocrat who interviews a long list of possible suitors for her daughter Gwendolyn. The man in this scene, Jack Worthing, wants desperately to marry Gwendolyn. Lady Bracknell interrogates Jack to see if he is worthy.

I was surprised Anh chose to play this British matriarch. It didn't seem natural for her to project her voice and chest in the assertiveness of 19th century aristocratic England. But she said she wanted "to learn how to do this."

Farid, about twenty-three, from Ethiopia, elected to play the role of Jack. He was a very sweet young man, and it was not a stretch to see him play the young suitor in love with Lady Bracknell's daughter.

I chose this script because the playwright Oscar Wilde did all the work for the actors and director with his brilliant writing. The power shifts start from the very first line of the scene with Lady Bracknell commanding, "You can take a seat, Mr. Worthing," and young Jack countering, "Thank you, Lady Bracknell, I prefer standing."

In the beginning of the scene, Lady Bracknell initially approves of Jack, his income, his residence, even his smoking habit. But confrontation increases when Jack is skirting the issue of his parents. The scene ends with the final line from Lady Bracknell: "You can hardly imagine that I and Lord Bracknell would dream of allowing our only daughter... to marry into a cloakroom.... Good morning, Mr. Worthing!"

I rehearsed with the students about twenty to thirty minutes a week. After several weeks, with only two weeks away from the dress rehearsal, the scene still wasn't working. Lady Bracknell refused to assert herself with her daughter's suitor.

"In my culture," explained Anh after rehearsal, "it's rude to speak that way in public. Also, in my family, my sister is the one with acting talent."

I felt my chest soften at her words. I knew she didn't need "acting talent" to be successful. Listening well and understanding the well-crafted script would do most of it. But she did need to assert her voice. Farid's character in the scene had a strong motivation to marry her daughter, and Anh needed to voice a strong opposition, or the audience wouldn't believe them.

"You can take a seat, Mr. Worthing...," Anh began, apologetic as always, swallowing the last syllable. Her eyes darted to the floor as she waited for Farid to speak.

"Okay, you guys," I said, standing up. "Let's take a break.

Anh, I want to try something. I want you to look away like you are doing, but keep your head high when you speak your lines and don't look at Jack."

She began her short interrogation of Jack by looking away, head and nose held high. It worked. I saw her aristocratic posture and heard a little bit of a bossy voice emerge. At this point in the script her character, Lady Bracknell, learns that Jack has lost his parents. Here she needed a new level of indignation: "I would strongly advise you, Mr. Worthing, to try to acquire some relations as soon as possible!" But while Farid continued to play his sweet, composed, and resonant Jack, Anh's voice trailed away again into wispiness.

I remembered, as an actor, how my directors used to run rehearsals. They kept running the scene over, asking the characters to move through their actions until some solution to a problem appeared.

"Anh," I said, "let's run the scene again, but when you get up out of your seat and Jack says he has no parents, I want you to hit the table when you say your next line. Can you do that? You know, like this!" I hit the table and said, "To lose one parent, Mr. Worthing, may be regarded as a misfortune; to lose both looks like carelessness."

She smiled at me, then giggled. And after I demonstrated, she even hit the table, the first time almost apologetically.

"Good. Try it again." I demonstrated another time for her and she followed me.

I also asked her to take two steps toward Jack as she said her lines. With these simple movements, assurance came into Anh. Her posture stiffened, her voice became more resonant, her volume rose. Jack reacted to her new vocal power by backing away from her, which was perfect. I relaxed and exhaled. We began to feel the play in action.

For their end-of-semester performance, I reserved a performance room on the first floor and invited my colleagues. The large carpeted room had a piano and many glass windows on the side. There was one row of faculty and two rows of my students. Some hovered nearby ready to help with a line if someone dropped one. Anh and Farid were the last go on. Anh stood tall, wearing a flowered hat and long dress, and she stuck her chin out. The room was quiet, the audience's eyes were wide, and they looked straight ahead at the actors. Some moments into the performance, my teaching colleagues, sitting front and center, even laughed out loud.

Anh gave one of the most complex performances I'd ever seen in my classes. It was as if the inner conflict of playing this character added to the interesting portrayal she gave. She had finally mastered the voice and the stance, but as an audience member you also sensed there was more going on in her as she acted this part. You were drawn to her. The students never gave in to giggles or laughter themselves, which made it possible for the audience to stay immersed in the drama.

At the end of the scene, Anh and Farid stepped to the center of the room and took their bows. Anh tried to stifle her giggles at the applause, but she was beaming and her fellow students and my colleagues were beaming with her.

"Integrated movement accommodates all learning styles..."[1]

Transformation Is Not All in Our Heads

In the book *Smart Moves: Why Learning Is Not All in Your Head*, neurophysiologist Carla Hannaford writes, "Integrated movement accommodates all learning styles, enhances myelination between the two hemispheres and balances the electrical energy and integrative processing across the whole brain." She explains that movement "is now understood to be essential to learning, creative thought, high level formal reasoning, and our ability to understand."[1]

I've seen this whenever my students bypass cultural beliefs or vocal patterns through purposeful movement in our play rehearsals. They get both their bodies and voices involved, especially in an atmosphere of creative play. They are suddenly able to short-circuit old patterns such as "it's not safe to be loud" or "when I talk, I cannot look a person in the eyes," such as Anh believed.

They are suddenly able to short-circuit old patterns such as "it's not safe to be loud"...

According to Andrea Isaacs, the inventor of Enneamotion and longtime student of the movement/mind connection, "We can relearn patterns by allowing outside matters to affect our inner neural pathways." Essentially, when we move in a new way, we let ourselves think differently. Actors train this way. "They use external stimuli," Isaacs reminds us, "like costumes or a gesture to affect their thinking, their reacting."[2]

Isaacs gives us a real-life example: sinking into a bathtub. We immediately have calmer thoughts and feelings. Our outer life influences our inner states. In purposeful movement, we begin to train the body to move into these inner states deliberately and help the brain create a new neural pathway. It's similar to cognitive behavioral therapy, which says: If you change what you think, feel, or how you move, you will automatically affect the other two. Or: If it's too difficult to change your thinking, then change something in your movement. Just a change in movement will change the way you react in the world and how you think about it.[3]

It's also true on the biochemical side. Hormones are involved in learning new things. Dopamine, the feel-good hormone, is released during pleasure and learning. GABA (Gamma Amino-butyric Acid) helps us block out other stimuli and focus on one thing. "GABA gives us the control to be fully present, mentally and emotionally, thus overriding the adrenalin reaction," says Hannaford in *Smart Moves*.[4] By doing the slow concentrated movements found in tai chi, qigong or Brain Gym®, you can stimulate the growth of dendrites from neurons that secrete GABA. You automatically increase GABA in the system.[5]

Alex Korb, PhD, a researcher at UCLA, writes that simple exercises like yoga or short aerobic movements, can boost serotonin levels as well. Serotonin can elevate mood and help with memory. I saw this every time we added purposeful movements to our rehearsals or warm-ups in class.[6]

Movement and Munni

Munni, from Cambodia, was a shy student of about twenty-four, with a gentle demeanor and voice. The role that he chose for his dramatic presentation in my speech class was Hally from *"Master" Harold and the boys* by Athol Fugard.

The play takes place in apartheid South Africa, and this early scene is light-hearted with hints of the class and racial conflict that will come later. Hally is a seventeen-year-old white South African boy and plays opposite Sam, a black South African man in his mid-forties. They are debating who is the greatest man who ever lived. The character Hally is a self-assured, overly confident, advantaged boy, so his body and his voice need to show this assurance for the audience to believe the conversation.

Munni approached the front of the class in rehearsal with his partner, Kwaku from Ghana, who played the older gentleman.

Munni began, "It doesn't have to be that way. There is something called progress, you know. We don't exactly burn people at the stake anymore."

Munni knew his lines and understood the historical references, but there was a problem: He believed in his bones that it was not polite to speak loudly, especially in a know-it-all tone. But he needed to do this to tell this story, and to allow the other actor to fulfill the role of calm humility.

"Munni, do you play soccer?" I asked.

"Sure," he said.

"Do you like to score goals?"

He grinned, nodding. Kwaku watched us, his forehead crinkling.

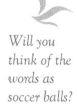

Will you think of the words as soccer balls?

"Will you try something just for fun? Will you think of the words as soccer balls?"

Munni gave me a blank stare, so I went on.

"I want you to try to kick a goal in the imaginary net over there next to Kwaku as you say your lines. Imagine you have to be quick and forceful to get it by the other players coming at you to intercept."

He shrugged his shoulders, gave a small kick, and spoke his line, "I don't know about him as a man of magnitude..."

A little more of his sound eked through as he occupied his mind and voice with movement.

"Good, now try it again and really try to score a goal." I stepped back to give him more room.

He tried a few more lines, kicking and talking, and within seconds words came out of his mouth strong and loud. Munni looked up at me with raised eyebrows.

"That's great, both of you!" I cheered them on.

With his bellowing soccer sound, Munni emerged into the room. And his partner, Kwaku, could now respond in a quieter way because this tone played well against Munni's loud voice.

They spoke a few more lines, with Munni kicking and Kwaku playing off his powerful sounds. We were all smiling by the end and having more fun. Munni's final performance was louder, though he had a little trouble duplicating the force of sound he had with the soccer kicks.

Brain Gym®

Carla Hannaford, author of *Smart Moves*, says that "learning comes in through the body and its senses first."[7]

In her book, Hannaford stressed the importance of physical movement and the Brain Gym® exercises developed by Paul Dennison, a pioneer in applied brain research. Dennison focused on connections between physical development, language acquisition, and academic achievement.

Research on the positive effects of Brain Gym® shows that "a coordinated series of movements, done slowly with balance, produces...a greater number of connections among neurons and even new nerve cell growth, especially in the hippocampus and frontal lobes of the brain."[8] These simple movements have been documented to show improvements in reading and math, and an increase in self-esteem and focus, among other factors. Many of these simple movements are "contralateral"—that is, they use arms or legs from opposite sides of the body moving together.

Exercises from Brain Gym®

Cross Crawl

One of my favorite Brain Gym® exercises is the cross crawl. I do this before tests, performances, or oral presentations. I have noticed that often there is a correlation between those students who cannot do this simple exercise and those who suffer severe anxiety or reading difficulties.

This exercise is short, easy to do, and can best be described as "marching in place." As your left leg rises, touch your left knee with your right palm. Then, as your right leg rises, touch your right knee with your left palm. It's important to do this exercise slowly.

Hook Ups

This exercise helps alleviate stress right away. When doing this exercise, be sure to breathe in through your nose and slowly out through your mouth.

Place the middle finger of one hand on your third eye (between your eyebrows, above the bridge of your nose).

Place the middle finger of the other hand in your navel.

Gently press each finger into your skin, pull it upward, and hold for 15-20 seconds. Often a spontaneous sigh or deep breath signals that the energies have "hooked up."[9]

Unexpected Benefits of Cross-Body Exercises

Emotional stressors in my life caused my short-term memory to fail me some years ago. It got so severe that I had to draw up detailed lesson plans for each two-hour class and cross off each activity after completing it in class. Finally I got an MRI, but the doctors found nothing wrong. (They didn't mention stress could be one of the culprits). At the time I didn't know how to help myself, and I tried many things: nutrition, alkalizing the body, therapy, and exercise.

About that time, I started going to a new gym in my neighborhood, which had thirty elliptical machines and little else. Elliptical machines require you to pedal while you swing your arms in opposition to your legs—opposite leg to opposite arm motion. This cross-lateral movement is the same type of movement found so beneficial in the Brain Gym® exercises.

I used the machines four or five days a week for thirty minutes each day.

My bout with memory problems disappeared after a few weeks; I returned to teaching and could make it through my two-hour classes without copious prompts. I felt such relief to have control of my mind again. I continued to go to the gym each week. After several more weeks of cross-lateral exercise, I felt less stress and sadness too—a side bonus. The few weeks of memory lapse seemed ages behind.

There may have been other factors as well, but this cross-lateral body exercise nourished my brain and nerve cells, and altered the stress response of the brain—in effect short circuiting the cortisol release. Long-term stress can actually shrink the hippocampus—the part of the brain that helps with memory. Short-term stress can also have a detrimental effect on memory retrieval and brain function. But the brain has great regenerative power, too. Cross-lateral exercise proved that to me.

Now when I see my students on hyperalert with fidgety feet and fingers, I know they will benefit from short bursts of movement to calm the brain and produce oxygen, to help bypass vocal and cultural limitations.

Tuning into rhythms is another powerful tool. We'll look at that in the next chapter.

CHAPTER 5

The Rhythm and Magic
of Shakespeare

I know a bank where the wild thyme blows,
Where oxlips and the nodding violet grows.
—Shakespeare,
Midsummer Night's Dream, Act II

My first teaching job was in a third grade class at the
Fayerweather Street School in Cambridge, Massachusetts. I was
in my twenties and not a natural elementary school teacher.
Kids need to know where their boots are, where they will
go at 9, 10, and noon; every activity needs to be organized,
planned, and practical. I didn't have adequate structure inside me to give them. I was not yet grounded enough in the
present—where children live.

I was reading the work of a British dramatist who had
reduced Shakespeare's words so that popular plays like *Macbeth* and *Romeo and Juliet* contained mainly the parts with
witches, ghosts, and sword fights—parts that could engage
kids. The language was kept in its original form, but plays
were shortened to about thirty minutes. I decided to try it
out with my group of twenty nine-year-olds.

The kids dug right in with the first scene of *Macbeth*: witches stirring brew. They imagined the gnarly witches bent over the stove and captured the mystery as they read their lines.

> Witch 1: *When shall we meet again*
> *In thunder, lightning, or in rain?*
> Witch 2: *When the hurlyburly's done,*
> *When the battle's lost and won.*
> Witch 3: *That will be ere the set of sun.*

We rehearsed it for several weeks and on a Friday afternoon performed the play in front of the whole school. The students had learned their lines well, and listened to each other for their cues. One boy, Louie, was otherwise often seen in a chair waiting to speak to the principal. Louie wasn't able to pay attention in class, and frequently got into arguments with other students. But in the play, Louie, in charge of sound effects, delivered the drumbeats and scary ghost sounds on cue. That Friday afternoon, all twenty children spoke all their lines and made their exits and entrances with perfect timing.

"When are we going to do Romeo and Juliet?"

A few days later, I saw Louie sitting outside the principal's office again. A teacher from another class had sent him there for getting into a fight. He sat on the carpet, his outstretched legs in the middle of the hallway. He looked up at me.

"Hi, Louie," I said.

His voice was sad. "Hi."

Then his eyes got wide and his voice got deeper. "When are we going to do *Romeo and Juliet*?"

"Do you want to be Romeo, Louie?" Children raced by to meet their parents in the parking lot.

"I want to be in the sword fight!"

I laughed. When we had talked about a sword fight in class, Louie had been especially attentive. "Great," I said, "you got it." He looked pleased, the sadness gone. A flurry of joy rushed through me as I went out the door to my car.

Rafe Esquith is an award-winning teacher who until recently worked at Hobart Boulevard Elementary School, an inner-city school in Los Angeles. For over thirty years, he rehearsed and performed a complete Shakespeare play each year with his class. According to a 2005 report on National Public Radio, all of his students were from immigrant families, and none spoke English as a first language. But these fifth-grade students consistently scored in the top 5 to 10 percent of the country in standardized tests.[1]

People came from all over the world to hear these students perform the play. I say "hear" because they focused on the language and used no costumes or huge sets. The children spoke the text clearly. Esquith's students have even opened for the Royal Shakespeare Company, appeared at the Globe Theatre in London, and were the subjects of a 2005 documentary film.

There is no magic potion, says Esquith, for acting out Shakespeare. The kids worked hard for many months after school and rehearsed many hours. They didn't overthink Shakespeare, just tuned into its rhythm, and according to actor Ian McKellen, a supporter of Esquith's work, did as well or better than most professional actors.

Anxiety or stage fright was not an issue. Esquith made sure that they knew mistakes are okay. "Some of the lines are still shaky," he said, "but between fellow actors onstage and others offstage, anyone who stumbles is caught by a dozen different safety nets." His students created a safe space so that if someone forgot a line, no one was angry. Instead, they worked together to find a creative fix. He adds, "Without the fear of 'messing up' the students rarely do."[2]

Because of this extraordinary learning model, many of his students beat the odds of their inner city environment and made it to the finest universities in the country. When they returned for a visit, they consistently reported that it was the theater production that taught them many of their lessons for success.[3]

William Shakespeare's work includes thirty-eight plays, 154 sonnets, and two long narrative poems. His plays have been translated into every major living language and they are performed more often than those of any other playwright.

Yet a lot of the language is older, the words unfamiliar. Why do students love it? Why does it feed them in this unique way?

Because of the rhythm.

Gifts of Rhythm

The rhythm of a good script is best caught through listening to it and speaking it out loud—not reading. Thought and emotion for the actor live in the sound of the words, the punctuation, the iambic pentameter, and the story.

Today's culture is more visual than the days of radio shows when the family gathered around trying to catch each word. Although podcasts have returned us to the aural experience, we tend to rely more on pictures, graphics, and screens. Younger generations who now text and tweet experience less face-to-face conversation where listening involves facial cues and body language: sensing the rhythms of communication.

But onstage, it's all different. To make a script come alive, we need to listen to our own voices, listen to others, and connect to the story.

Last year, I experimented with this in my classroom, using scenes from *The Tragedy of Richard III*, *Othello*, and *The Merchant of Venice*. Each scene I picked was rich with conflict and stakes were high, so I knew the students would engage with the drama.

As an actor, I had memorized Portia's mercy speech for auditions years before. Speaking the words "The quality of mercy is not strain'd. It droppeth as the gentle rain from heaven" showed me rhythm. When I let my voice relax into this rhythm, the meaning of mercy actually vibrated through me.

I hoped the rich text of Shakespeare, the high stakes, and the rhythm of the pieces would fuel my students, too.

When I let my voice relax into this rhythm, the meaning of mercy actually vibrated through me.

Helene, a seventeen-year-old girl from Haiti, was the youngest in class. She slid in each night ten minutes early and sat in the back row, close to the door. While others chit-chatted, she kept her gaze on her books and cell phone. She wouldn't participate in class discussion unless I called on her. Then she always had the right answer.

I had a nudge to give Helene Portia's mercy speech because Helene had written about ethics and justice in other assignments. She took the script from me slowly, scanned it, looked up dazed. "Ma'am," she asked. "What is she saying?"

I knew Helene attended a religious school on the weekend, so I asked her, "You know mercy from your Bible studies? Portia is asking for mercy from this lawyer because she loves the man they are trying to execute. And you have to dress up as a man to act as his defender."

Paul, another timid young man, would play Shylock. He had only a couple of lines, because he was reading a poem as well, but he would be onstage with Helene so she was not alone.

My other Haitian student, Jacques, would play Othello. Jacques stood 5' 11" and looked almost 250 lbs. He always sat in the farthest corner of the room, away from everyone, scowling, but he liked to volunteer to speak in front of the class. I paired him with Rose, from Colombia, who played Desdemona.

Rose was earnest in her studies and strained to understand me in class. But she never volunteered to read in front of class, only in small groups. Rose and Jacques were polar opposites.

At our performance, Othello (Jacques) came to class with a hat and a black shirt and pants to mark the special day; his wife, Desdemona (Rose) brought a pajama top to wear over her jeans to depict the bedroom scene.

"Kill me tomorrow," cried the shy Rose. But as her words couldn't change the course of Othello, her jealous husband, he took the small pillow I had brought from my house and pretended to snuff out her life.

"Yet she must die," intoned Jacques, "else she'll betray more men."

We all leaned forward in our chairs; we didn't want to miss a beat. Jacques had found the rhythm in Othello's words and it was breathtaking to hear the lines.

They got up quickly after the death scene for their bow. I looked at the other students in the room who were clapping enthusiastically.

"I never was on the stage until today," Rose told me afterwards.

"How did you feel?"

"Nervous." She gulped a breath.

"But you did it today, Rose," I said. She nodded, looking down at her books but smiling.

Helene appeared in a Florida Gulf Coast University shirt. Her long black hair was tucked into a baseball cap. She had dressed as a male athlete to defend her love in court against Shylock.

Her partner Paul, the youngest, shyest student, worked two jobs. In one of the few rehearsals he was able to make, I had told him, "Please be loud and angry, so that Helene has a reason to give her mercy speech. Can you remember a time when you were angry?"

"Sure," he grinned shyly.

"Try to speak the lines with that anger."

He did. Paul stood strong in front of the class, facing his partner Helene, and bellowed in a deep voice, "On what compulsion must I? Tell me that!"

As demure Helene began her speech, she threw her right arm toward the ceiling and her left hand against her heart. She looked up at the sky, as if in her argument for mercy from the heavens. "The quality of mercy is not strained," she cried.

Her voice rippled through the room. We held our breaths until the end when Helene took a quick bow and moved with wide strides back into her seat in front of me. She found a power in her voice from exploring the rhythm of this passage with her whole self.

My class was more connected after this day of performances. Helene began to strike up conversations with me and others and spoke more in group discussions. Paul and Jacques changed too. Paul's face seemed more relaxed. Jacques no longer wore a scowl in the back of the room.

Several weeks after the semester had ended, I met with Rose, the woman who had played Desdemona. Over lunch in the noisy cafeteria with televisions blaring news in the background, we discussed her career goals. "Rose," I told her, "you did so well playing Desdemona. You captured her emotion perfectly."

"But the words," she replied, shifting in her seat. "They were so hard."

"You found the rhythm and the meaning. We were convinced you were innocent in that scene with Othello," I said.

Students filed by with trays of food. Rose looked up from her sandwich. "I did stop worrying what others thought of me." Her head tilted in thought.

"And you read out loud a lot more after that."

"That's true." She looked up, her eyes sparkling. "I wasn't afraid after that."

Rose was no longer afraid, because she had finally grasped the rhythm.

The rhythm in language, once you catch it, can teach you and move you in astonishing ways.

How I Work with the Rhythm of Shakespeare

Rhythm allows us to understand meaning and motive. Rhythm and great writing stirs the imagination so that fear doesn't take over. This rhythm is in ocean waves, the seasons, our breathing, our heartbeat. There is even a rhythm in teaching a class.

The rhythm in language, once you catch it, can teach you and move you in astonishing ways.

Ben Crystal, author of many books on how to use Shakespeare in schools, connects the rhythm of Shakespeare to our living pulse. "Iambic pentameter is the rhythm of our English language and of our bodies—a line of that poetry has the same rhythm as our heartbeat," he says. "A line of iambic pentameter fills the human lung perfectly, so it's the rhythm of speech."[4]

In my classes, we start with the basic storyline. "This is a story about a husband and wife," I'll tell them. "In this scene, Othello thinks his wife has slept with his best friend. So, in this scene he's furious and kills her. Can you imagine such a strong emotion?" The students discuss this, and they get more familiar with the concept of the play. Then I read the script with them in small groups. We rehearse every other week and they repeat their lines out loud, over and over, with partners or with me.

We talk about the conflict and the subtext too. If they want, I record my own voice reading their part. The more they practice it out loud with others, the more they hear the rhythm, catch the meaning.

Ken Ludwig, author of *How to Teach Your Children Shakespeare*, began reading Shakespeare to each of his children when they were in the first grade. "You can't pretend to act Shakespeare without knowing how to breathe, listen, interpret, and pace yourself. Mere emoting won't cut it," says Ludwig. "And here's the thing: Shakespeare actually tells you how to say his lines right in the text, as long as you know how to read it properly."[5]

Oscar-winning actor Michael York believes that the characters know exactly what they want. Actors learn who they are portraying by the details in the plays, but also by the sounds, the language, and the rhythms.[6]

To me, Shakespeare is pure rhythm, pure structure. Structure is what I needed to give my elementary students in my first teaching job, and I found it in Shakespeare's

"A line of iambic pentameter fills the human lung perfectly, so it's the rhythm of speech."[4]

Macbeth. Structure and rhythm helped Helene and Rose tap into the emotion and meaning of the words in *Othello.*

"Shakespeare was rooting for a kinder, gentler humanity," Ludwig shared in an interview. "Once we start understanding him, we become better people because of it."[7]

CHAPTER 6

Using Props, Costumes, and Sound for Transformation

The art of letting go of one persona to be in another's shoes requires discipline and focus. Finding this level of authenticity can be a mystery even to the actors playing the role. Sometimes it comes through the actor's training, talent, or voice. Sometimes it arrives through the help of props and costume.

Most great actors use props and costumes to help them discover the different aspects of their characters. I think of how Daniel Day Lewis's Lincoln transported me back to Lincoln's world of difficult decisions. Meryl Streep played such a convincing Margaret Thatcher that Thatcher's authorized biographer, Charles Moore, claimed in a recent interview after seeing the movie, "I thought I was looking at her (Thatcher) at times."[1]

He wanted to understand how the path of acting served as a path to personal freedom.

Psychologist Brian Bates studied with actors from the Royal Academy of Dramatic Art for seven years. He wanted to understand how the path of acting served as a path to personal freedom. In his book, he recounted many stories of transformation, but my favorite was how

Marlon Brando prepared for his screen appearance with director Francis Ford Coppola, for Don Corleone in *The Godfather*.

"Brando penciled in the mustache and began blackening his blond hair," writes Bates. "He added some dark makeup under the eyes and stuffed tissue in his cheeks to give himself a jowly look.... Coppola produced a plate of apples and cheese, and poured a demitasse of espresso to serve as props."

At that point Brando put on his worn shirt, tie, and old jacket and lit an Italian cigar. His belly suddenly extended and his shoulders sagged, his face grew waxen and his breathing got heavy. When the telephone rang, "Don Corleone lifted the instrument and placed it slowly to his ear. He listened, nodded slowly and patiently, and then replaced the telephone without a word. Whoever was on the other end heard nothing but the heavy breathing of an aged man." Marlon Brando had become Don Corleone.[2]

In an interview on NPR, Meryl Streep spoke about her role in the movie *Doubt*. She played a nun who brings allegations against a priest, and the interviewer asked Streep about her conservative plain costume. How could she change into her character, since there wasn't much she could do with such a dull hat?

"Oh no," Streep contradicted. The hat wasn't dull at all. There was so much she could do with it. She could tip it down in the front a little bit or to the side.[3] That one prop opened up a world of possibilities.

Streep also spoke about Colleen Atwood's costume designs for the movie *Into the Woods*, and how the costumes affected her acting. "Some of the most productive character work was finding what [Atwood] was telling me about the character through the clothes," Streep said. "She thinks like an actor—how the change would be for the witch, how she blended me into the gnarled everything, things you can't even see, but I knew about, just where the costume stuck into me and made me miserable, that was all character."[4]

Many of us know the experience of putting on a favorite dress, an expensive suit, or a tuxedo and how it changes us. Like Brando's cigar, maybe it's the final touch of earrings or a special pair of cuff links that were handed down from someone that makes our bodies stand a little taller, that makes us move more gracefully.

A Doll's House

One afternoon I was rehearsing a scene from *A Doll's House* with three students. It was a few weeks into the semester and I wasn't sure if they could relate to Ibsen's 19th century Norway. In this play, the husband, Torvald, treats his wife Nora like a child, calling her "my little skylark" and "my little squirrel." He claims his love is true, until the end of the play when Nora gains strength and demands he take her more seriously, and the marriage dissolves.

In this early scene, Nora's childhood friend, Mrs. Linde, newly widowed, has come to ask Torvald for a job. Torvald has the authority in this scene.

Marie, a student from Ghana in her twenties, played Nora, and nineteen-year-old Adele, from Iran, played Mrs. Linde. Neither one could embrace their characters: Marie giggled after her line, "Poor Christine, you are a widow," while Adele preferred to whisper her lines: "Yes, it is three years ago now." Mengestu from Ethiopia played Torvald but fumbled his lines and couldn't come in on cue. He was more concerned about getting a job in his real life.

One afternoon in class, I stood in a circle with the three of them. We'd had a bland rehearsal. "This is an old-fashioned play and it's formal," I said. I knew it would help them feel the characters if they dressed up a little bit. "Adele and Marie, you'll need to wear a long skirt or dress. Do you have something like that?" Adele nodded and Marie just smiled. I wasn't sure if she was in agreement, but I decided not to press the issue.

"Mengestu, can you wear a formal shirt?" I asked, trying to read his reaction.

"Do I need a tie? I can wear a tie, too, if you need."

"That would be great." I leaned back, relieved he was eager and open.

We rehearsed a few times over the next three weeks, but the students changed only slightly. Adele began to speak more loudly but Marie still slouched and swallowed her lines, while Mengestu seemed distracted. They hadn't tried their costumes yet; they were still just learning lines.

I took Mengestu aside one afternoon. "Everything going okay with you?"

"Oh—I lost my job." His voice trailed off. "I'm looking for a new one."

It was definitely affecting his performance, but I asked him to keep me updated. Each time we rehearsed, the three students absorbed more of the subtext from Ibsen. I found a pipe from an ex-smoker friend for Mengestu and gave it him.

Then, ten weeks after working with the group for only twenty to thirty minutes a week, it was final performance day. The students were focused on getting ready, some changing into costumes, adding a hat or makeup, others reading through their scripts for last minute reminders. The air felt electric with a mix of excitement and nerves.

Marie and Adele were the first to go to the front of the classroom. Marie still spoke softly, swallowing the endings of her words, but Adele was strong. She had found a long black skirt and dark high heels, and the costume created a stiff and demure posture, perfect for Mrs. Linde.

As they began their scene at the front of the class-room, the class was attentive to Mrs. Linde, convinc-ing in her role. Nora held her hand on her hip more like a 21st century twenty year old than a 19th cen-tury aristocrat.

The two finished reminiscing about the old days and it was Torvald's cue to enter. As Mengestu stepped into class from the hallway into the front of the classroom, now the stage, I heard gasps from the student audience. He wore a white pressed shirt, dressy pants and tie, and held a pipe. His walk had completely changed. He strut-ted across the floor towards the ladies, aged and taller, in control of his wife and his world.

Mengestu's pipe, his starched white shirt, and his swagger helped both him and the audience. He spoke in a patronizing way to his wife and wife's friend. I had nev-er seen this character until he put on his costume and held his pipe. Students were turning to me, nodding and smiling, as he delivered his lines clearly. The scene ended and the three actors took a bow, while we all clapped.

A hat tipped just so, a necktie, or a particular set of heels, sets a character change in motion for the actor and the audience. A costume or a prop works its way into the subconscious and affects what an actor does and says. And even more is possible: When students practice these kinds of new perspectives in the classroom, their adopted attitudes can spill over into the rest of their lives. Mengetsu got a job before the semester ended. Af-terwards he told me he thought that acting that charac-ter helped him change his outer life.

A costume or a prop works its way into the subcon-scious and affects what an actor does and says.

Props Stimulate the Imagination

One semester in speech class, we decided to tackle the one-act play *It's Not You* by Craig Pospisil. The comedy is set on the New York subway. Three friends are breaking up with their fourth friend. It's fast-paced banter that moves quickly between players, like a ping-pong match.

Khalid from Somalia played Nathalie, Tsegay from Eritrea played the one male, John, Cristina from Argentina played Amber, and Elizabeth from Mexico played Terry. After several rehearsals, progress felt slow. The students understood the humor of the play but couldn't capture the rhythm of the quick New York dialogue. One of the ladies was supposed to be pregnant but couldn't alter her walk or posture. I thought about what was missing.

Then one week I added props. I piped in a recording of a subway train. I asked the students to sit or stand as if on a subway, swaying to the sound of the cars on the track. I gave Cristina a small pillow to put under her sweater to show her advanced pregnancy. She began to hold her lower back as if to support her body. The other players reacted too, making room for her, inviting her to sit.

Students who stood up pretended to hold onto the imaginary loops of metal hanging from the train ceiling. Tsegay snapped his gum loudly. The sounds of the subway and the swaying of bodies helped create the boisterous mood of the city. The more they focused on the sounds and their props, the less inhibited they were. They sped up their dialogue. By day's end, the students were attentive, smiling, eager to perform the next week for their class.

By using props that gave them something to do, their attention was directed outwards toward communicating with each other.

Altering place, sounds, or costumes can alter one's state of consciousness.

Props Can Aid Anyone's Transformation

Every class feels like a performance for me, and I wear my costume and carry my props, too. I have to know my lines, the curriculum, and dress the part. I hope that my audience will hear me, interact with me, and respond. My props may include my briefcase, a stapler, comfortable shoes, black slacks or skirt, and a pocketful of chalk or dry erase markers. These props, their feel and purpose, bring me into the mindset of my job.

One semester, I had a challenging group of students. The class was required for their degrees, but they strolled in late and were slow to open their books or get to their seats. Every creative activity I tried failed. When I wanted to play music to show them something about rhythm and language, the video wouldn't work. When I assigned homework, they complained. If they didn't do well on tests, they challenged my grading.

I tried everything to try to turn the class around: I posted homework ahead of time, offered extra credit, stayed late to tutor. But it didn't work.

Then I had an idea: I brought a rock with a personal word of inspiration carved on it. I put the rock in my pocket every class. It weighed little, but I always knew it was there. I held it when I wanted to focus on my love of learning, teaching, and higher ideals.

That tiny prop shifted my attitude and affected my actions, helped me change a negative situation into a more positive one.

Gradually, I saw changes. That tiny prop shifted my attitude and affected my actions, helped me change a negative situation into a more positive one.

In his book *The Way of the Actor*, Brian Bates writes about the big transformation that can occur with just a small shift like my rock. "A physical transformation powerfully affects the way we experience ourselves," he says.

69

"And the ways in which others respond to us."[5]

Holding something, or using our hands and body to interact with a prop, propels us into a different world. Sometimes students learning how to express themselves in a new way become introverted and self-conscious. They start thinking too much instead of doing. But if they can put their hands on a prop or wear a large heavy hat, or stand and sway on the New York City subway, it helps them let go of their own anxiety to be in the present moment.

CHAPTER 7

Imaginative Techniques

Summer semester had started, and the trees were leafed out now. I pulled into the parking lot of a college where I'd taught one class before. I had just resigned from my elementary school and was unemployed with no other prospects. Today was a job interview for a full-time teaching position.

I tried to collect my thoughts, but my mind and emotions were in turmoil. Three days earlier we had buried my grandmother, a key cheerleader in my life. She was the one who always tried to rally me. One of her last letters had carried me through a series of lonely times: "Dear, dear Thérèse, another step has been taken. One that took courage, spirit, and self-reliance. . . ." Her words always settled on me like a cozy quilt. She knew how to make me feel more courageous when I did not. I had been unable to read a poem at her funeral. The knot of pressure around my throat had robbed me of a clear voice.

She knew how to make me feel more courageous when I did not.

I sat in the office of humanities at this college, watching students walk in and out to talk to the secretary about

71

a scheduling conflict or a grade. My knees were pressed together and hands lay on my lap, my mind busy going over interview questions. Family mourning and difficulties over the days of the funeral had exhausted me. And this job was a stretch for me: I knew I had to act as if I could do it, because I didn't have the PhD or years of experience of other candidates.

Before sitting down, I'd headed for the restroom to do my breathing and vocal exercises. I stretched my spine and released my jaw, freeing tension. I stood in front of the mirror, practicing an easy smile and a grounded straight-back stance. I pulled my hair back again to put the stragglers in place. I straightened my stiff white collar and plucked the last cat hairs off my dark suit. I had worn pants every day to teach sixth graders, but today I wore my only suit.

A faculty member led me down the hall to the conference room where the other committee members sat around a table. I took the one empty seat and said hello to everyone. I sat up straight, legs crossed, and lowered my voice so that it wasn't filled with my "wanting to please," high-pitched breathy voice. I allowed my breath to roll through me as I sat in the hard chair.

I allowed my breath to roll through me as I sat in the hard chair.

The five administrators and faculty on the panel asked me a laundry list of questions. Although I was still probably firing off cortisol and adrenaline, the vulnerability from losing someone I loved allowed a more authentic me to emerge. The stories I told about my life and teaching flowed out easily, as if they were about someone else: how I had managed thirty-seven twelve-year-old inner-city students for a year, how I learned to work with a diverse population here and abroad. I talked about the "portfolio approach to writing" as if I had used it for years, when I had only learned of it a few days before. I spoke of assessments as if I knew them inside and out, when I had used them for only a semester. I was acting as if I could do this job, ignoring any doubts which surfaced.

I was the last of twelve candidates to interview for the position. As I left the interview I knew I had done well, was relaxed and able to answer each question in the interview. I also knew the competition had PhDs and more teaching experience. I went home to think about my next steps. Where could I live if I didn't get this job? How would I find work? Could I stay in the apartment I'd just rented?

A week later I got a phone call with the job offer. Relief ran through my whole body. After unpacking some boxes, I finally slept. Acting "as if" had worked—with a little help from my late grandmother.

Acting "as if" had worked…

Many of us feel like imposters in such situations. In her TED talk about body language, Amy Cuddy tells her story of her years in graduate school after she'd had a serious head injury that caused brain damage. The doctors told her that a college education was not possible for her after her injury. But she kept at it, she said, faking it until she made it.

The end of the faking came years later, when she was teaching at Harvard. One of her students broke down in her office. "I don't belong here," the student told Cuddy. The student felt like an imposter, but Cuddy knew that her student did belong at Harvard. Cuddy herself had been practicing "fake it till you make it" for so long in her higher education positions, her confidence had become a deep truth. She was no longer an imposter in her own mind. "You are going to do it and do it and do it," she told her student, "until you become it!"[1]

That's the formula for using the creative imagination to become what you dream. In an experiment Cuddy did with a colleague at Berkeley, they set out to determine if nonverbal communication influenced how we think about ourselves, not just others. She decided to look at hormonal shifts (specifically cortisol, the stress hormone, and testosterone, the dominance hormone). One of her assumptions going in to the experiment was that powerful leaders have high testosterone and low corti-sol—they are good at reacting to stress. So she and a colleague brought people into the lab and asked them adopt "high-power poses" or "low-power poses" for two minutes. The results were revealing: High-power poses brought a 25 percent decrease in cortisol whereas the low-power poses brought a 15 percent in-crease in cortisol.

Just as my high-power pose helped my job interview when cortisol levels normally spike, Cuddy's experiment showed lower cortisol amounts in people who did the power pose before a job interview than those who did not. Not only did the cortisol levels decrease, but the judges in charge of pick-ing the job applicants preferred to hire those with high-power poses. To Cuddy, this was not an artificial situation: she be-lieves high-power poses helped the job applicants to express their true selves. The behavior, the movement, changed the attitude of both the person doing the exercise and those who witnessed it. "You have to have the experience, do it, to then become it," Cuddy concluded. "Our bodies can change our minds, and our minds can change our behavior, and our be-havior can change our outcomes."[2]

Years later, a colleague who had been on my job interview panel admitted to me, "You blew us away in the interview, Thérèse." I wasn't quite sure if she was complimenting my acting skills or my teaching, but by then I was a long-time faculty member and had earned the real-time teaching skills to not care.

"You're Not a Writer"

Once I secured this new position, I had to actually do the job of teaching reading, writing, speaking, and grammar to college preparatory immigrants. Where reading and speaking were within my comfort zone, writing and grammar were far outside it. Since seventh grade, I had repeatedly told myself I was not a writer.

I remember one Friday afternoon during an English test. My friend Mary nudged her elbow first against Katherine's and then against mine for the answer. I fell for it; Katherine didn't budge. When I looked over at Mary and her paper, our handsome English teacher caught me.

I was lanced in the gut. I said nothing. I loved this teacher and was so ashamed he thought I cheated. His knowing voice pegged me a fraud, and it stifled me for years.

My mother, a frustrated journalist who didn't get to pursue her career, wanted to help me with my papers. Her lifelong goal of writing and her printed words, elegantly carved, outshone my own. Further proof to my teacher, and to me, that I was incapable of writing well.

So there I was on the first day of the first writing class at my new job, with twenty-five students ready to learn writing from me, a fraud.

I could hear my nylons scratch together as I approached the front of this new college class. I lay my books on the desk.

Beads of sweat collected on my forehead, and I clung tightly to the edge of the desk to prevent myself from tipping over. An electric clock hummed on the wall. My students sat there, with their blank tired stares, waiting.

I picked up the chalk, breathed deeply so that my shaking hand could settle and I could write my name on the board. My chest was trying hard to contain the overactive beating of my heart. I wrote my name on the board. I added the name of the class. Done. Only two hours and thirteen minutes left.

For years, I experienced this kind of terror every day in the classroom. I hid it from students and other faculty. The only way I got by was to act "as if." Actors and athletes often use this imaginative principle to accomplish their goals or score a touchdown.

Each day I dressed and acted the part of a writing teacher until one day the skills and confidence showed up.

Each day I dressed and acted the part of a writing teacher until one day the skills and confidence showed up. Stacks of papers and inspirational quotes lined my office cubicle. I had learned a guttural language like German to access more sound, so I could alter my voice and posture to make myself feel more confident. I didn't wear jeans, because it sent a message to my brain that I could have been gardening. I asked my students to call me Ms. in the beginning of my career. I took other writing teachers to lunch and tried to find what they did, how they taught, moved. I listened to them speak to their students.

A way out of fear is pretending—acting. Pretending can bring us to our imagination. We imagine that we can lift ourselves out of fight and flight. When we pretend, we leave some negative emotions behind. And when we pretend with an audience that rewards us, the brain releases dopamine, and what was initially pretend becomes joyful.

These tools of imagination helped me get through that first semester of writing classes at the college. And after several semesters, I learned that I didn't need to know everything. As long as I provided opportunities for students to practice writing and experience feedback in a safe environment, they would improve.

The writing traumas I experienced as a teenager also helped. I tried to teach students to look at what they were doing well, along with what they needed to improve. I knew from personal experience that negative emotions interfered with the ability to produce on the page.

A Further Example of "As If"—Thinking from the End

The simple act of standing up and speaking in front of others for two or three minutes, several times in a semester, changes a student's brain. On the first day of each semester, I ask my classes to visualize themselves at the end of the semester, encouraging them to make a wish list, where they write down what they want to see from themselves by the end of the semester. I also visualize my class. I visualize a comfortable setting, where students feel like they can take risks. I visualize my own relaxed body posture. I know that if I am fearful or disturbed, it rubs off on the class.

With this end goal in mind, I create a syllabus where students in the oral communication classes, for example, have six to eight opportunities to give a short presentations. They hold a vision for their success. With such a positive end goal in mind, new ideas or fun exercises come to me often. My own creativity is sparked by a good visualization.

One semester I worked with ESL students in a beginning speech class. These students, new to the country,

(S)tanding up and speaking in front of others for two or three minutes, several times in a semester, changes a student's brain.

had little experience in public speaking. In the first two weeks, they sat in groups speaking their native language, hesitant to volunteer. I asked them to visualize what they wanted at the end of the semester and think about the steps to get there.

One of the steps was to give speeches, to keep having more and more experiences, as Amy Cuddy proposed, until the experience itself transforms. Week three, I asked them to give a speech on their dream home. To prepare, we made a large circle. At first these students didn't even want to stand up. I pushed away the chairs to create space, until they finally joined me in the circle.

Sonia and Maria, both timid students, stood closely together, glancing sideways to make sure the other was still there. We did short improvisation exercises (see chapter 17) as they worked around the circle: first, simply counting off in the circle, then making a sentence in English by adding one word to the previous person's. Finally, they improvised a story together. At the end of the exercises, Maria's face had relaxed. Sonia was watching the rest of the students, her arms loose by her sides.

The next class was the day of the talk. We started with qigong breathing and shoulder shrugs. I had them warm up using notecards. In this exercise, they stood in front of the class and only had to make a simple sentence but they had to use the word on the card and make eye contact.

They were anxious beforehand, talking excitedly in their native languages of Spanish, French, Creole. "This is about having the experience until it's real," I told them. "You practice as if you can do this, until you can."

Sonia and Maria left with smiles after their presentations, as did many others. These two students even started to come early to each class to try out their new skills. They were motivated by their small successes, and each received an A on her talk.

An Extreme Example of the "As If" Principle

John Corcoran offered an extreme example of acting "as if." He was a high school English and history teacher who couldn't read beyond a third grade level himself. Originally from New Mexico, Corcoran made it through high school and college with a full athletic scholarship.

Corcoran's students were interviewed about his effectiveness as a high school teacher. They claimed he gave them more opportunities to read out loud (since he could not) and peer review each other's papers. His students also talked of how he cared for them, and they knew it.

Corcoran says he went into teaching because it was an easy field to get into. But he also said it was because he wanted to help children like himself. He had ideals about education, and hoped he would learn to read if thrown into a teaching environment.

His "as if" principle came about through the coping strategies he developed. "I learned my lines and acted out my part like an aspiring young actor on a movie set," he said.[3]

Today John Corcoran can read and is apologetic about his hidden past. His reading tutor encouraged him to share his story of illiteracy. He has become a well-known advocate for literacy, working with presidents Clinton and Bush. The nonprofit literacy organization he began in California has been active for almost two decades.

Often our greatest struggle can lead to our greatest service. John Corcoran relied on his imagination to get through his years as a teacher. His greatest struggle became his greatest teacher and source of inspiration for others.

What if our deepest fears and insecurities are doorways to our best service and creativity? When I think of that, it makes it easier to take each challenge as an exercise of the imagination.

WHY ZARMINA SINGS

Exercise for Greatest Service

Think of a longtime fear or obstacle you have had. Write without stopping or concern for grammar for about ten minutes on this struggle. Then write for another ten minutes on your secret dreams. How are they related?

Imagination is not just a fun tool to rely on in the classroom. It can rescue us from feeling alone. When we begin to use it in our lives to help us "visualize an end goal" or "fake it till we make it," we can tap into our own unique way to serve in the world.

In chapter 4, imagination helped Munni "kick" his spoken words as if he were kicking a soccer ball. It changed his physical demeanor, outlook, and voice, giving him confidence. That exercise came easily to me. But what about those times when you are brought to your knees by a class and have to dig deep for an imaginative solution? Our next chapter explores this.

Exercises to act "As If":
Try These with Your Class

Tell students: Think of something you'd like to do or be. Maybe you'd like to be thinner, or maybe you'd like to be a writer. Maybe you'd like more confidence or more wealth. List ten attributes of people who have these attributes or successes in their lives. What would it be like to think like them? How do they dress? How do they walk? Write fifteen to twenty of their attributes.

80

CHAPTER 8

The Horse Whisperer

I sat slumped at the teacher's desk that I'd moved to the hallway corridor for my midterm conferences. The hall offered less traffic and more privacy than the classroom, so I chose this option rather than cancel that afternoon's class. Inside, my students were watching the documentary *Buck*. We had been reading an autobiography of writer Louis L'Amour, and I wanted to show them a cowboy of today. But I also hoped the authentic beauty of the movie would ignite something in these students. The class had become disjointed and disconnected, and we all needed some motivation or inspiration.

It was a challenging group that term. Twenty-six-year-old Mayra, with her long black hair and a far away look, always arrived late to class. Randall preferred to doodle skillful cartoons on his girlfriend's notes rather than discuss the college prep essays. Young Kebede sat alert following the discussion threads, but could not refrain repeatedly sidetracking into a loud long-standing argument with the man next to him, who was from Sierra Leone. Yure, so afraid of failing his courses, but so used to using others' assignments as his own, had to visit the dean after his third offense to get a better appreciation of the college policies on cheating. And Hicham, in the front row, kept his eyes down on his desk and rarely spoke to anyone.

At one point, six weeks into the spring semester, I had left the room in frustration and headed to the water fountain to get a drink while the class worked on an assignment. Who did these students think they were? Why were they always testing me like this? When I finished my drink and looked up from the fountain I saw a male student down the hall. He was pushing the door to the women's restroom. I stopped him midway. "Excuse me, I think you're going in the wrong door." He pivoted back toward me, startled, rereading the sign. "Oh sorry," he said. "I didn't know where I was."

As I walked back to my hallway desk, I thought about this. Maybe the students in this particular class didn't know where they were. Maybe they were sorely in need of clearer signs, more boundaries or classroom rules, and more motivation.

I sat down and waited for the first student to appear for her conference. The new twist in my gut now had two sources: I had to fail eleven out of twenty-three students at midterm—an all time high for this reading class. And also, I needed to dig deeper into my own resources to find motivation for these failing students.

Horse Whisperer's Wisdom

The subject of that documentary, Buck, is a real-life horse whisperer. He travels around the US teaching people how to trust their horses. In the process, the riders learn to trust themselves. This new awareness and sensitivity heals both the horse and the person. "It's the process of him learning and me learning at the same time," Buck says. "You think of [you and the horse] as one mind, one body."[1]

In one scene in the movie, Buck attempted to break a palomino stallion. This stallion bit and kicked; nobody could approach it. The horse's owner had removed any natural order by raising the stallion in her own house—even bottle-feeding it. The horse never learned to respect other horses because he was never given the opportunity to learn the ways of his species. The woman also kept seventeen other stallions in the same field: a situation completely out of balance.

Buck greeted the palomino with a relaxed but exacting discipline. There was no fear in Buck, but a quiet calmness as the horse tried to buck, bite, and disobey. He was direct with the owner. "What is it you are trying to prove?" he asked her when she resisted his comments about having better boundaries and discipline with her horses.

The film's soundtrack filtered into the hall where I waited. I thought about my own teaching and the reaction I had to these students. When I moved too quickly with lessons and requirements, it caused the students anxiety. Some began to carry on loud personal conversations, and some shut down. Others, like Kebede, argued nonstop, or like the silent brooding Mayra, became suspicious of my motives.

Like Buck, I needed to be clearer in my requirements and consequences for behavior. I needed to adjust my curriculum to meet the needs of this class, because each class was unique. As I sat there I realized I'd grown afraid of some of the students. Fear had shut down my creative abilities.

Fear had shut down my creative abilities.

The result was this midterm day when I had to meet with every student in this concrete hallway to give him or her sad news.

Mayra came out first. I motioned her to sit. I decided to see if she would open up. "Is everything going okay?" I began. "You seem to have trouble focusing in class." She looked up slowly to see if I was really talking to her.

"I can't really think about class right now." She shook her head, tears in her eyes. "I need help."

I thought of the counselor I knew at the school. "I know someone who can help you," I said, handing her the counselor's phone number. "I trust her very much. Will you go see her?"

Mayra let out a big sigh and nodded, relieved to have shared part of her story with someone.

As each student arrived, I thought of how Buck might approach them. First, point out strengths and weaknesses, outline for each what they would need to do to turn things around. One needed to complete the homework, another needed to study for tests and read, others needed to do all the above. Most of the students listened and seemed relieved to know.

Only one student contested her grade. "I don't understand why I failed."

"You'll need to read, do the assignments, and pass the quizzes," I told her matter-of-factly.

"Oh," she sighed.

Kebede came outside for the conference. "Thanks for showing that movie!" he effused.

"What did you think of it?"

"I never saw a cowboy like that."

"I never saw a cowboy like that." He sat down in the chair, and we talked easily about his grade and his study habits. He was the last student, so I collected my papers and we returned to the class.

The movie had ended, and music played as Buck

performed a gentle dance on his horse going backwards in figure eights. I watched the students who sat still, mesmerized by the beauty of the picture. Some discreetly wiped tears away.

As I walked to my car that day, I was exhausted, but my arms were swinging without the weight of worry or the bags of exams.

At home, I put my feet up and looked at the treetops out my apartment windows. It was mid-March and new buds were appearing. I reflected on the class with a new perspective: I had faced my worst fear, failing half of these students, and I had lived through it. I had also shared something I loved—the beauty of Buck and his dance with people and horses. Buck's wide capacity to build trust had changed us all that afternoon.

We Learn by Teaching

I walked into our next class meeting and dropped my books on the desk. Twenty-three students were in their seats, eyes on me. The wall clock said 1:00 p.m. and I knew I was in the correct room, but it felt different. Everyone was present, attentive, listening.

"We have eight weeks left and a lot to do," I began. "I'm going to make some changes in the curriculum. Each of you will teach one chapter of the novel, with a partner, to the entire class. Here are the lesson plan instructions." They sat quietly as I passed out the instruction sheet that showed class objectives, and a sample lesson plan.

"You'll need to give the class a short quiz at the end of your lesson to make sure they learned the material. Our final exam will be a collection of these quizzes."

I set up times to meet with each pair of students so that I could go over their plans and their roles, to be sure they felt confident enough to try this.

The final research report would now be an oral presentation—either a dramatic reading or a group skit where they created dialogue in a reader's theater format from a part of the book. The dramatic reading would eliminate accidental plagiarism, because they would have to invent dialogue based on the character.

I knew that the pressure and excitement of performing something in public—whether from a lesson plan or a dramatic reading—would inspire them to rehearse and learn the materials. I also gave some deadlines for each step of the process: a date to meet with me, a date to write their rough draft of their presentations and lesson plans, a date to teach the lesson and present.

"Any questions?" I picked up the extra papers and stacked them in a pile.

"Who do we work with to teach the chapters?" piped up Yure.

"I've made small groups for that assignment," I told him, and read out the groups. They quickly turned to the two or three people in their groups to exchange email addresses and began to plan their lessons. I let out a long easy breath and sat back in my chair.

I thought again of the calm wisdom of the horse whisperer: "A lot of it is being creative," Buck had said. He called good horsemanship simply creativity. So much of teaching was being creative, I realized now, and when my students got creative, they got more involved too.

As it came time for students to stand up and teach, I didn't hold back from adding movement and vocal work. I did my favorite vocal warm ups with them, like calling and the yawn/sigh. By week eleven, when I forgot the vocal warm up, one of the students reminded me, asking if we could do the "yawn stretch thing."

The assignments to teach took the burden off me too. I no longer had to force them to read. They wanted to read, to learn the material well enough to teach it. And they remembered it when it came time for their final exams. By experiencing the material in multiple ways, it was more easily stored in their memory.[2]

A Final Breakthrough

A final breakthrough came with Randall, the Japanese American student with the penchant for doodling. A few times after class, he had charged to the front of the room and sat down in my chair as if it were his own. The first time I laughed it off. The second time he did it, two weeks after midterm conferences, a light went on for me. "Do you want to be a teacher, Randall?" I asked him. "Well, yeah," he said shyly. "I've thought about it, but it seems too hard."

When Randall delivered the lesson on his chapter, he was the strictest disciplinarian of any of us. He did not hesitate to call on someone who was not getting involved. I saw that he was a natural teacher.

Buck Brannaman knew how to build a bridge to his students using the horses, and moving past fear into good communication. We teachers also need to be able to ride past fear into creative territories, while we establish trust and boundaries.

By final conferences, I only had to fail one student. Mayra was not able to pull up her grade enough to pass; however, she spoke to me of her plan to get help to balance her personal and academic life. The challenges of home were still affecting her learning.

After my experience with this class and our transformation, I got curious about the affects of trauma on people. I knew many of my students came from very difficult backgrounds. It

87

wasn't until after this class that I met a very special soldier and an equally special therapist, and learned about the reality of trauma and how it affects learning.

Chapter 9

Trauma and Learning: What Do Soldiers and Scientists Say about Anxiety and PTSD?

I met Bryan Brown when my husband and I were looking for a financial advisor. We got to talking. I mentioned that I was researching the effects of anxiety and PTSD (Post-traumatic Stress Disorder) in the classroom. Bryan had been a soldier in the Middle East and was very concerned with what was happening to military men and women after their tours of duty.

It can be unreal, he said. "I was firing my weapon in Iraq on my last tour," he told me, "and seven days later I was sitting on my parent's couch watching TV." Back in his hometown, with such acute memories, he had trouble listening to people in line at Starbucks complain about their lukewarm coffee or standing in Walmart trying to choose between sixty-two different deodorants.

In his eight years in the military, doing tours in Kuwait, then Afghanistan and Iraq, Bryan has been hit by three IEDs (improvised explosive devices), a car bomb, and sniper attacks. His last tour was the worst, and after it, Bryan opted for no psychiatric treatment even though the experience was traumatic. He just wanted to return

"I was firing my weapon in Iraq on my last tour," he told me, "and seven days later I was sitting on my parent's couch watching TV."

back to his "normal life" and didn't want to talk about what had happened to him.

He lived with "his head on a swivel," he said, unable to relax or sleep, trust the moment or people, or focus for long periods of time. He often could not fall asleep till 1:30 a.m. and was up again by 3:30 a.m.

Bryan finally reached out to the Veterans Administration, after his wife urged him to seek help. Counselors there helped him recognize triggers that made his PTSD worse. Some were smells such as the hand sanitizer they had used in the Middle East. Others were as simple as sitting in a classroom "being scored." Being scored was a trigger because it was a timed situation where survival was based on performance in that moment. These triggers would propel him back into combat—into that "time capsule" where the explosions or combat took place, where his brain went into fight, flight, or freeze.

Since I was particularly interested in stress in the classroom, Bryan told me that he learned to deal with it in two ways. The first method was breathing. He would breathe and count to ten, trying to let the tension go. His other strategy was unique, something he still uses. "I always kept an Army Commander's Coin on my desk in the classroom," he said. "For some strange reason, it helped me focus when I looked at it. When I looked at it, I remembered that things would be okay. I have been in much worse situations."[1]

Bryan's success in returning to his "normal life" after battle was impressive. He not only came to terms with his past, but he went on to complete his business degree and excel in his current position.

I knew that many of my students exhibited signs of PTSD or ADHD (attention deficit hyperactivity disorder). The number of students in the United States who have PTSD in one study was found to be just under 10 percent in colleges,[2] and higher for at-risk populations such as combat soldiers or traumatized refugees. PTSD and high anxiety are widespread among refugees forced to leave their countries because of war, but can even affect those students who have left loved ones and familiar surroundings to learn a new language and culture. Feelings of isolation can trigger stress reactions.

Interview with a Therapist

Not long after my interview with Bryan, I met Kristin Towhill, who worked with veterans suffering from PTSD. Kristin offered to help me understand the time capsules that interfere with learning for trauma survivors. We met one day at a Starbucks near her home.

We settled in at a large round table near the windows. "People suffering from PTSD have these time capsules of the memories which contain triggers," Kristin began. She had a youthful appearance, short, cropped brown hair, and alert but welcoming eyes. "These triggers remind us to go into the state that we were in at that time, which include the physiological response of fight or flight or freeze, as well as the emotions and thoughts or any other sensory data, such as what we were seeing or smelling at the time, or the physical pain. The more emotional intensity there was, the more easily it's triggered. You need to work with these networks of memory—the thoughts, emotions, and physical reactions."

"These triggers remind us to go into the state that we were in at that time...."[3]

Sensory data. That reminded me of the hand sanitizer that set Bryan off in his story. She explained more: that the time capsules are memories in our brain that contain the inner and outer environment of what was happening to us in that moment of trauma.

"The beliefs are also stuck in our brain," Kristin said, "in our short term memory. Such as 'If I fall asleep, I'll die,' or 'I'm never truly safe.'"

Bryan's "head on a swivel" response seemed to fit some of these descriptions.

"Some of my students have told me their traumatic experiences of war or being a refugee," I told her. "I see this intensity of emotion. A kind of hyperalertness triggered by stressful situations like speaking in public." She nodded. "I've felt it in myself too."

"I see this intensity of emotion. A kind of hyperalertness triggered by stressful situations like speaking in public."

People moved by with their coffees. She went on. "We now know that these beliefs can likely lead to self-blame or more negative views of ourselves, others, and the world. Once explored, we find these beliefs were useful to get by at the time to maintain safety, or to help the person to continue to feel in control. But in order to heal, we need to find some way to feel safe again, even though we are never entirely in control of what happens to us."

"How do you help these veterans feel safe again?" I asked, thinking of my students. A sense of safety was vital to learning well.

"I use multiple methods starting most importantly with a kind, calm presence, then offering tools based on the client's interest or skill deficits," she said. "For every person, I start with educating them about what they are experiencing and why, which leads immediately to teaching them to work with their breath. Breath can interrupt the buildup of the panic response, and I use a catch phrase: 'Wherever you go, there you're breathing.'"

Such similarities between her treatment and what I employed in the classroom! "I'm amazed at how things often come back to the breath in the classroom, too," I said.

"If they are ready to commit to confronting their pain in order to change their lives," she said, "I offer evidence-based therapies, which means treatment modalities [methods] with the most research behind them, proving not only that they work for PTSD, but that they offer a standardized, systematic approach. My favorite evidence-based therapies are EMDR (eye movement desensitization and reprocessing), cognitive processing, and prolonged exposure therapy."

So many approaches! I scribbled notes.

"When we've been traumatized, we flood our bodies with stress chemicals, like cortisol, that continue to float around, strengthening the ongoing feelings of stress, fear, and anger. And the more the actual feelings or responses are avoided, shoved down, or walled away, the more strongly they come up in our bodies."

We paused for a moment as she nibbled her snack. Kristin spoke with passion; I wrote fast to keep up.

"The very first drive of any living being is to stay alive. The second is to avoid pain," she continued. "When considered in this manner, people with unhealed trauma live constantly in a state of feeling they are in immediate danger, and of reliving, on a myriad of levels, the worst experiences of their lives. The biggest threat to themselves and society — such as hostile behavior towards others and self-endangering behaviors trying to avoid pain—come when people are not yet aware that they are being entirely driven by an unconscious need to protect themselves from relatively nonexistent danger and entirely internal pain."

I thought about my own journey. Before I had been able to accept, feel, and be aware of my own anxiety, I had definitely developed coping strategies to avoid my own pain. One of the less destructive patterns was my constant travel, moving to different cities and countries. I ran from job to job and place to place.

I interrupted her. "Do you have any thoughts of what a teacher in a classroom can do?"

"You can help them be aware of the trauma coming up physically, and develop more internal awareness, by prompting them to share any physical sensations that arise as they think about or discuss certain issues. The more awareness they can develop of their own responses, the more feelings of control they will have, to identify anxiety or anger, or any other emotion, as it arises, and deal with it appropriately."

Already, I had tried to acknowledge students' panic by stopping class and doing breathing exercises. I asked them to tune into their bodies before a speech. I purposefully helped them move out of the head into the body.

She continued, "The goal of the therapist is to help someone broaden their awareness, so they can stay calm and connected to their bodies and their environment even while they are accessing painful memories or emotions. The experience of getting lost in a painful experience from the past as it happens in therapy is called 'abreaction.' When someone abreacts, they are being retraumatized. They are no longer present as their rational selves to be able to learn from the experience.

"Helping someone to escape this continuum means using our calm presence, the skills we teach them, and the positives that we elicit from them, such as their beliefs and feelings of love, to also access other memory networks, to 'straddle both worlds,' otherwise known as dual awareness.

"If a person can spend enough time practicing skills, such as examining beliefs about their trauma—thoughts like 'it's all my fault my friend died'—to help them to break down the time capsules into smaller elements, the beliefs can be filed away in more positive, adaptive, memory networks," she said.

I looked at my watch and saw that our hour had flown by. My head was buzzing with information.

Before we parted I asked her about how long it took to heal from PTSD. Was that possible for the soldiers she worked with?

"If I noticed someone is triggered during the assessment I'll teach them the deep breathing in the very first session. Many of them have said that's the most relaxed they've felt in years, so there's already a change in the very first visit. When we're doing the evidence-based treatments, people can see a noticeable difference after just five or six sessions. Most of the treatments go for about 12 sessions once or twice a week, and the majority of patients no longer fulfill criteria for PTSD by then. Pretty cool huh?"

We finished our snacks and got up to leave. "The successful completion of this process is experienced by survivors as a feeling of achieving resolution," she added. "It's often described as 'finding my peace' or 'coming to terms' with it."[3]

Bryan Brown had mentioned coming to terms with his experiences in battle in a similar vein. He had focused on the positives just by gazing at his coin, felt relief being able to speak candidly to a therapist who listened.

That semester, I tried some of Kristin's ideas in class. I had been very impressed with both Kristin and Bryan's emphasis on deep listening and the "kind calm presence" Kristin tried to have with her own clients. So before each presentation, I tried to foster this. I would both calm myself and give each of my students some words of encouragement: "You're going to do great today," or "You've been practicing, so I know it's going to go well."

You can feel nervous and still give a good talk.

Before their final presentation, I added a few new warm-ups. The students were used to the qigong breathing and shoulder shrugs, but I asked them to also notice where the tension might be in their bodies. Was it in their gut? Their chest? I asked them to breathe into it.

"I have butterflies!" cried Marie. It was a subtle change, but it sparked interest in a few other students.

"Just notice them," I told her. "Anybody else find a nervous place in their body?"

I saw nods as I scanned the room. "Just breathe into those areas. Notice them, and let them be. You can feel nervous and still give a good talk."

I saw this new awareness of tension, and the positive calm feedback I gave about it, slowly alter their expressions. They felt the sense of safety, which led easily to a sense of accomplishment.

The wounds of the past can heal. I was grateful to Kristin and Bryan for sharing their journeys, for the work they did in recovery, and their generous spirit to give back what they learned.

In my classes, I give students difficult situations: oral presentations, scenes to perform. These situations trigger stress. But by creating safety for students in such high-stress situations, they can face the feeling of trauma and fears and create new outcomes.

I began to see parallels in what Kristin Towhill did with her clients and what happened in my classroom. Creating a calm and engaging presence was a delicate balance, but it could be transformative.

CHAPTER 10

Just Breathe

A week before my first semester teaching college preparatory English full time, I sat at my desk looking over my student lists—seventy students signed up so far. I had classes in speaking, reading, and writing, five credits each. Only five spaces left to fill. These classes would keep me busy. I sighed and got to work on the syllabi. As I was finishing one, a colleague poked her head into my cubicle.

"How's it going so far?"

"Good," I said, trying to neaten some of papers strewn all over my desk. "Just wondering if someone has a syllabus on this reading course from a previous semester."

"I can get you one." She smiled, then added, "Do you mind teaching one more class? It does make your course load twenty credits, but the good news is it's the same preparation as your other writing class."

I swallowed. "I'm not sure." I wanted to be a team player. I wanted to make a good first-semester impression. But I didn't know how I was going to teach one more writing class.

She kept going. "It's the same prep as your other writing class—you won't have additional preparation."

"All right," I stammered slowly. "I can do that."

"That's great. We appreciate it. You know you'll need to introduce the students to the same four rhetorical modes of writing."

What was a rhetorical mode? I kept hearing that term all week long in meetings with other teachers. What did I just say yes to? Who could I ask for help? I couldn't talk to anyone about my fears. I had to appear to know what I was doing. As my colleague walked away, I did the math. Another class would bring my load to almost a hundred students.

All the following week, my brain and body were running a habitual pattern of fight or flight. In my case, my brain was stuck in flight mode—I multi-tasked, running quickly between activities, mentally chewed on the same thing over and over. I'd had panic attacks since my early twenties, and though they had decreased in frequency, this kind of stress triggered them.

As I speed-walked to my first class, I heard the hurried voices of students behind me. My breathing was rapid and shallow, but I was too tense to do anything. I just grabbed my handouts from the printer and continued down the stairway to the classroom.

My twenty-three students were all present but not all in their seats. It looked like a circus. Some were talking over each other; others were buried in the music of their iPods. One student, whom I came to know as Sardor from Uzbekistan, was balancing on the back of his chair while his feet rested on the seat.

I put my books on the table in the front of class, said hello, forced a smile, and quickly walked back out of the room.

The restroom was empty. I stared into the mirror. A pasty-white fearful face stared back. My breathing was still quick and shallow. I felt pressure in my head and noticed sweat on my forehead and palms.

"Oh my God, what am I doing here?" I took a gulp of air and counted to four on the exhale. At first there were no thoughts, just a feeling of wanting to run. My heartbeat seemed to quicken and there suddenly wasn't enough space in my lungs for breath. "Oh my God. I'm having a panic attack."

I forced myself to breathe and be still. I allowed the pangs in my chest and stomach just to be there. As the panicky thoughts arose, I returned to the physical sensations in my body and to breathing. With each breath, feeling began to return to parts of my body—my feet, my arms. My chest softened a little. Suddenly I was no longer the victim of my horrible thoughts, but the watcher of these thoughts. As I watched my panic, the thoughts turned to an energy that rolled through me wave after wave. It all happened in a matter of moments.

I felt vibrant, electric, as if the fear were just a tight ball of energy that needed to circulate.

I felt vibrant, electric, as if the fear were just a tight ball of energy that needed to circulate.

After just three or four minutes, I ambled back to class. The students were all seated in their chairs now, eyes upon me as I walked to my desk. Sardor, now in his chair, looked up at me, wide-eyed but calm.

We got to work, and I made it through that first semester, even with a hundred students.

I had been practicing breathing and being present with the panic attacks ("practicing presence" as it is called) for a couple of years. The breathing was a key component. I noticed that my own calm affected my students: If I was stressed out, my students were too; if I was relaxed, class seemed to flow.

Carla Hannaford, in her book *Playing in the Unified Field*, talks about mirror neurons. We have mirror neurons in utero and after birth. They help us learn how to "mirror" the world around us to develop those hand gestures and facial expressions that let us communicate with the world around us. Mirror neurons are also thought to contribute to our ability to express emotions and have empathy for others.[1]

A calm cooperative classroom appeared more regularly, usually when I loved the material I was teaching that day. But it also happened when I became aware of my breathing, not focused on the "worry loops" in my mind.

I began to use breathing techniques more and more with my students, too.

Teaching Students to Breathe through Their Fear

I noticed a curious phenomenon among my students. On days when we had group presentations, group discussions, or rehearsals for group performances, my students arrived on time, pulled out their books and papers, and eagerly got together with their small groups. They focused on the assignment and each other.

But a darker side came forward on test days. Whether it was the simplest twenty-word vocabulary quiz, a three-question reading comprehension quiz, or the midterm exam, even outgoing students entered the room speaking in hushed tones, sweaty palms clutching their books, down-trodden looks tossed my way.

They seemed to scream at me with their eyes, "How could you do this to us!?"

We need to test. We need to review material, find out what stuck and what didn't.[2] But even when students embraced movement, voice, and props as part of the class curriculum, they could fall into panic with anything that tested their knowledge on paper.

I knew that under certain emotional stresses, when the brain and body are engaged in fight or flight, students were less able to process problems, remember details, or make decisions. Their minds had trouble gaining access to higher level thinking processes.

I decided to put my own learning into practice, see if it might help once again. Like movement, breathing can short circuit the cortisol and adrenaline output and bring calm. It helped me think on my feet and energize a class. Would something as simple as breathing on a test day work?

Would something as simple as breathing on a test day work?

Just Breathe, Qigong Style

I had studied qigong (*chi kung*) with Chunyi Lin, in Minnesota. In his twenties, Lin was forced into labor camps as a victim of the Cultural Revolution in China. He had wanted to end his life more than once, and he healed himself of depression, joint pain, and other ailments through qigong. The breathing exercise I learned with him is the one I began doing in almost every class I taught.

"When oxygen becomes less available to the whole body due to constrained breathing," writes John Loupos in an article on deep breathing, "your brain experiences the effects of oxygen deprivation just like the rest of your body. Any or all of these symptoms can then both reflect and/or reinforce your body's chemical and/or hormonal imbalance, causing serotonin levels to decrease and cortisol to increase, further complicating this debilitating cycle."[3]

One of my most challenging groups was a reading class that started at 1:00 p.m. just after lunch. One day, I had gobbled my own lunch at my desk, as always, and ran up the flight of stairs. I dropped my books on the desk, arranged my papers, handed back some papers, and turned on the computer. Most of the class was missing; only four drooping students sat in front of me.

I wrote something on the board to kill a few minutes and eight more students dribbled in. We got out our novels, and I passed out paper. No one responded. One young man with coffee was staring wide-eyed out the window, at motionless trees.

"Okay," I said, deciding it was time to try my theory. "Could everybody stand up?"

They looked at me, then at each other.

I motioned with my arms. "Karen, Madeline, can you stand?"

A few courageous students stood. The others slowly followed.

"We're going to do a little breathing. Hold your arms out as if you're holding a beach ball. Like this," I demonstrated. "Now breathe in and open your arms. Okay. Now, even more slowly begin to close your arms as you exhale. This is qigong breathing; it's good for the brain."

After three repetitions of this exercise I noticed they all seemed to be standing taller. Their arms hung more easily by their sides.

"Now, let's try a shoulder shrug. This is simple too. Just breathe in and bring your shoulders to your ears. And exhale slowly letting your shoulders fall. Let's do this three more times." As we did this, most of my students began to smile. I saw more energy in their faces and eyes. And when they sat down, I felt more energy circulating in the room. We launched into the lesson, and it was a good class.

It only takes a minute to breathe but the changes can be dramatic, whether you are preparing for a presentation, trying to reduce panic, or get the glucose in your body to reach your brain. I do these exercises regularly now before a presentation or exam, or whenever the students look tired. I can see the results right away in their eyes.

After I breathe with my students, there is an awareness of each other that wasn't there before. Breathing together reminds us that we are not alone.

Breathing together reminds us that we are not alone.

Anxiety, Hormones, and the Brain

I gave a training recently on using movement and drama in the classroom. Before starting my presentation, I was extremely nervous—my heart was beating, and I started to shift into panic. But this time I knew what to do. I had a few minutes, so I went outside and did the breathing exercises, along with some Brain Gym® exercises like hook-up and cross-crawl as described in chapter 4. Energy started to flow.

Anxiety affects our ability to retain information and think more deeply because it causes the body to produce higher levels of cortisol and adrenalin. Dopamine, the neurotransmitter released when we're learning, dips as adrenaline and cortisol rise.

When we go into fight or flight, the stress signal, either real or imagined, stimulates the hypothalamus to release hormones, which then tell the adrenals to fire off glucocorticoids, according to Robert Sapolsky, a neuroendocrinologist at Stanford. One of these glucocorticoids is cortisol. The body needs cortisol short term for energy. But when cortisol keeps producing without rest, problems arise. These stress hormones can damage the memory and other functions in the brain and body, Sapolsky says.[4]

Long-term stress can affect the hippocampus's ability to download short-term memories into long-term memory. The hippocampus is worn down by excessive amounts of cortisol in the bloodstream.

Each time a learner (or a teacher) faces new material, this flight or fight response can kick in.

Each time a learner (or a teacher) faces new material, this flight or fight response can kick in. Breath, like contralateral movements (cross crawl), helps us turn off the stress response. In my classes and in myself, I was seeing how the simple act of focused breathing could help create new circuitry in the brain. As this occurs, new opportunities for learning open up.

Breathing Exercises

Shoulder Shrug

Raise your shoulders up to your ears, inhaling deeply. As you exhale slowly, slowly bring your shoulders down. Make sure the exhale is almost twice as long as the inhale.

Qigong Breathing

Hold your arms in front of you like you are holding a beach ball. As you breathe in, widen your arms slowly, to your side. Next, as you exhale, slowly close your arms in front of you so that you are at the starting position of holding the beach ball. Do this three  times. Generally, you will see the shoulders of the students drop after the first round.

For more on this method, see Chunyi Lin and Spring Forest Qigong.[5]

CHAPTER 11

Slow Down

I arrived at my basic level writing class that day fifteen min-
utes early. I balanced my briefcase on the metal chair, took
out my markers, and wrote on the board. *Today: new materials,*
partner work, reflection writing, group work. Every minute of the
eighty-minute class was accounted for in my plan. I was excited
by all we would accomplish.

Students walked in slowly, took their seats, bleary-eyed
from fighting traffic and working all day. "We have a lot to
do," I said as I rolled up my sleeves. I hoped for the same
results with this group that I got from my summer semester
of advanced writing students. They had shown so much im-
provement, and I was sure we could do the same in this basic
writing class. "We've got a few minutes to put the answers
for this exercise up on the board, and then we can talk about
elements of an introduction."

A couple of students got up and sauntered to the blackboard to share the responses from the exercises. Some looked
bored, so I tried to speed things up even more.

"Great job. Now let's finish up this chapter, so we can get
to the test on Monday."

When class ended, the group flew out the door. Only Maura stopped to ask me her grade, again.

A few weeks into the semester, I noted more students were trudging in late. Several were even failing to turn in assignments and talking about their Saturday nights in their groups instead of the class work. Most were only getting Cs and Ds on the chapter quizzes.

One night in class, I overheard Roberto mumble to his partner, "I am so lost!" I looked up. Other students were grumbling in their group discussions.

Maura, my serious quiet student who always sat in front, suddenly yelled, "Cucaracha!" The cockroach, half-dead, was hobbling down the carpet in the middle of the room.

Roberto got up, walked over to it and stomped on it. "Thanks, Roberto," I told him, forcing a smile.

Stamping out the cockroach just seemed to punctuate the lack of coherence in this class. And my approach didn't capture their attention. The students looked for distractions.

I thought about the previous summer's class. We had tackled a chapter a week and the group still did so well on the tests and writing. This group was nothing like that group, I lamented. And then it hit me. They weren't like that class because these students were four semesters behind that group's level! I was moving too fast.

I went in the next day only a few minutes early, placed my books gently on the table, and wrote just two items on the board. I sat quietly in my chair by the computer waiting for the students to arrive. I checked my watch, told myself, "Be patient."

Students started trickling in.

"We're going to go back over sentence structure from the last chapter, and review that today," I told them.

I gave the group time to get out their books, turn to the right page. "Does anyone want to explain the compound sentence compared to the complex sentence?" I stayed in my seat and looked around the room.

A couple of moments of silence followed. I fought my urge to break in and share the answer. Finally, Maura raised her hand. "The compound sentence is one sentence that has two independent thoughts?"

"Yes. Can someone give an example from the exercise on page 91?" The clock on the wall kept ticking, and I waited till someone came up with an example, just breathing.

I slowed down everything that day: my response time, my explanations. I went over every point at least twice. I threw out the timetable I had planned. It didn't apply to this group.

Within about two weeks, things changed.

Roberto got his first B on a quiz. Maura seemed to smile more and ask less frequently about her grade. More students were passing than failing now.

Julian Ford and Jon Wortmann assert: "To step back, to slow down, activates the frontal lobes. It's how we can send the first signal to our alarms that everything is all right."[1] By slowing down, giving students more time, I gave them the ability to process and avoid fight or flight. Research shows there may be a connection between moving too quickly and going into stress.

In his podcast "Desirable Difficulties: Slowing Down Learning," Robert Bjork, research professor at UCLA, discusses the benefit of slowing down class material to let it seep into students' long-term memory.[2] He refers to a study done by Mary Budd Rowe in the 1970s. Rowe coined the term "wait time." She discovered that teachers waited an average of 1.5

seconds for students to respond to questions. If they waited at least three seconds, there were more benefits: Students got the correct answer more often, and said "I don't know" less often. Teachers increased the quality as well as the complexity of their questions.[3]

Positive Benefits of Slowing Down for Athletes

When I think of tennis star Serena Williams, I see someone who is not in a hurry. When Williams waits for a serve, her muscles are taut, her feet shift side to side, her eyes are fixed on the server across the net. She is ready for the 100-mile-an-hour serve, which could land with a topspin, slice, or flat speed. But she is not rigid or hurried. She moves with a balance of relaxation and tension, open and poised so that she can turn on a dime and return the serve. To me, she looks like a relaxed spring, ready to jump in any direction to reach a shot.

In Serena's match against Victoria Azarenka in the 2013 US Open, she won the first set easily. But she began the second set making many errors. I noticed her eyes didn't lock with the ball the way they usually did, and she was hitting it a moment too late or too early. Between points, she yelled at herself after making an error, her head down, frowning. Her face lost the neutrality she had had in the first set. She lost the second set and was down in the third set.

Then I saw her make a deliberate shift. Her head and demeanor steadied. She slowed down! She looked straight ahead and walked more slowly, even shortening her strides between points. She took deep breaths. Her serves began to hit inside the lines of the service court. She changed the flow of the match by changing her own pace, and ran away with the important final games of the third set and match.

Slowing Down Helps Us Empathize and Connect

Slowing down is medicine for calming an anxious brain and body. It allows time for students to find an answer, but it also creates opportunities for compassion and deep thinking. In his Pulitzer Prize-nominated book *The Shallows: What the Internet Is Doing to Our Brains*, Nicholas Carr writes, "It's not only deep thinking that requires a calm, attentive mind. It's also empathy and compassion." He cites Antonio Damasio, director of University of Southern California's Brain and Creativity Institute, who discovered that "the higher emotions emerge from neural processes that 'are inherently slow....' The more distracted we become, the less able we are to experience the subtlest, most distinctively human forms of empathy, compassion, and other emotions."[4]

Slowing down is medicine for calming an anxious brain and body.

I'm certainly less able to connect to others when I'm in a hurry. But slowing down activates those mirror neurons discussed in chapter 10. I saw this in action last year when I did my first Skype teaching presentation with adjunct faculty who wanted to learn how to use dramatic techniques and movement in the classroom to decrease anxiety.

My students were a thousand miles away in a college classroom in Virginia. When we finally connected on Skype, I struggled to make out the faces on my screen. "Is everybody there?" I asked. No response. Then moments later, I heard jumbled comments like "We're here, Thérèse." But when I tried to connect to them, the camera on the other end only showed me rows of tables and people's legs and waists. Any facial expressions were hidden.

At first, because of my anxiety, I sped up my speech, not able to wait for them to respond on the other end. I could feel my heart racing, my panic growing.

Then, everything shifted. About fifteen minutes into the presentation, I started demonstrating the qigong breathing technique I use with my students to help them relax. I stood, keeping an eye on the tiny red dot on my computer and opened my arms wide for the qigong breath. I exhaled slowly and closed my arms in slow motion.[5] After three breaths, my shoulders came down and my breathing slowed and deepened. We synchronized our breathing and I began to slow down naturally. My sentences came more slowly. I was able to direct my attention out toward them for the first time in the presentation.

The workshop progressed through the improvisation exercises. As I moved into the comedic improvisation, I could hear the faculty laughing with each other as they did their role-plays. The voices on the other end got louder and more energetic. They were mirroring my change and finally enjoying themselves.

The coordinator who organized the training on the other end noticed a change after the qigong exercise, too. "We all felt more relaxed and connected with you after that breathing exercise," he said. "Everything slowed down."

Chapter 12

Pay Attention!

A lot of what acting is, is paying attention.
—Robert Redford[1]

In *The Shallows: What the Internet Is Doing to Our Brains*, Nicolas Carr blames the Internet for some of our new struggle to pay attention. We have huge numbers of "competing messages" that "overload our working memory," he says. Because it's primarily the frontal lobes of our brain that we need to focus attention on something like learning, Carr says that "memory consolidation can't even get started. And, thanks once again to the plasticity of our neuronal pathways, the more we use the Web, the more we train our brain to be distracted.... Our brains become adept at forgetting, inept at remembering."[2] Not ideal for classroom productivity or enjoyment!

What can solve our new attention deficit? The arts, including theater. In my classrooms, distracted students turn their behavior around through drama and movement.

Sir Kenneth Robinson, bestselling author and education adviser, adds that we can learn more easily through the arts because they address "aesthetic experience...[when] your senses are operating at their peak, when you are in the present moment, fully alive."[3]

111

Karim was in my oral communication class years ago. Our class met in a white-walled small room with metal chairs, a cement floor, and one window. Karim was about twenty-five, and he spent long moments looking out that window. He was constantly multitasking: trying to make a living at night, going to school during the day, and sending money home to his family back in Tunisia.

When I called on him in class for his opinion, he often stumbled. Unable to follow the thread of most conversations, he was always one week behind with his homework and scored below 50 percent on most tests. When I asked to see his notebook, he showed me a manila folder overstuffed with papers from the three classes he was taking. I spoke to his writing teacher and learned he demonstrated the same behaviors in her class: failing grades and distraction.

He came to me after class one day, holding the latest test he'd failed. "I need to pass this class!" he said, hands outstretched. "Please tell me what to do."

Students were starting to file in for the next session. "Can your boss give you different hours that will work better with your class schedule?"

He looked down at his shoes then back up at me. "I'll ask. I don't know."

Later that day, we met in my office for the short time that he had and I did my best to organize Karim's notebook. "Did you like any of those scripts we read earlier in class, Karim?" I asked him. He closed his notebook, looked at me. "We read these three." I held them out to him. "Was there a part you liked most?"

His eyes landed on the shortest play. "This one looks good."

"All right." I picked up the script and handed it to him. "I think you'll like this scene. You'll be a father talking to his daughter about the difficulties of being a parent and working."

112

The play he had chosen was *Tender Offer* by Wendy Wasserstein, with a scene both humorous and sweet. I wasn't sure he'd be able to memorize the lines of the play or make it to rehearsals. And I was right. I tried to rehearse with Karim and his partner, but we found only a couple of opportunities. He hadn't memorized the lines, so we weren't able to explore the emotions of his character or add staging. Instead, he read from his notes.

On the day of his performance, Karim showed up in a dark blue business suit to play the part of the tired businessman. "Great costume, Karim," I said, but quietly clenched my teeth, still worried about his performance.

His turn came, and Karim walked tall onto the stage—the front of the classroom—and sat down at the table. The room got quiet. I saw that a switch had somehow turned on inside this young man. Within seconds, Karim took out his newspaper, sniffed at an imaginary cigar, put his feet up on the table, and sipped from a coffee cup. The picture he created of the harried businessman, troubled by the pressures of parenthood, are still imprinted on my mind all these years later. I was propelled into his kitchen, his morning, his world.

His daughter strolled onto the stage. "Daddy, what do you think about?" she began. "I mean, like when you're quiet, what do you think about?"

He looked up at her from his paper. "Business, usually. If I think I made a mistake or if I think I'm doing okay."

Karim shared his worries about the world and his financial future, and his partner shared her life in college. The scene was so real, the actors so connected, that we smiled when he joked about paying for his daughter's tuition. By the end, the daughter had succeeded in getting her father to look out the window at the shapes of clouds that looked like "Walter Cronkite and elephants dancing."

The scene ended. Karim stepped confidently to the center of the room with his partner for their bow. I gave them both a "great job!" From that moment on, this attention-poor student started to pull his grades up. He was able to pass my class that semester, and his speeches and performances during the second half of the semester were strong.

How did Karim remember his lines, staying 100 percent present, when he could not retain content from a book or be present in a classroom discussion? What magic happened for him onstage that day?

According to Adele Diamond, a neuroscientist, the classroom cannot be a passive place. Students need creative play or drama to help stimulate the part of the brain that helps a person stay on task. Creativity also increases executive lobe function because it requires memorization and social interaction. Diamond believes that the prefrontal cortex is responsible for our ability to stay on task when we're bored. It also is the place for working memory, being able to think outside the box, or switch ideas—out of which comes good planning and problem-solving.[4]

Karim's prefrontal cortex seemed very active as he engaged in this final dramatic project. His attention became specific and focused, so much so that he drew all of us into his performance. Success with attention onstage gave him confidence to stretch himself in other areas of the classwork.

The Mindfulness of Acting

Psychologists Helga and Tony Noice looked at how actors remembered their lines and found that it is not through rote memorization but through breaking their script up into separate intentions, called beats. Then actors focus on what they want, the details of the scene, and listening/reacting to the other actors. They engage more of their brain and body.[5] Mindfulness training for actors has led to more spontaneous performances where actors can be present and pay attention to what is happening around them.[6] They naturally retain the words and don't have to memorize. Most actors don't want to memorize their scenes by simply plugging in their lines to their memory: it gives a lifeless performance.

Years ago, I played Grace from *The Faith Healer* in a small production in Seattle, WA. Written in 1980 by Irishman Brian Friel, the play is about three Irish actors roving the Scottish Highlands in the early 20th century. They recount the highs and lows of their adventures in separate monologues. Grace is on the verge of a nervous breakdown but can't see it in herself. Her opening lines begin with the string of Scottish towns her troupe has performed in: "Aberarder, Aberayron, Abergorlech."

During this thirty-five-minute monologue, I chain-smoked marshmallow cigarettes, drank refills of colored water that resembled scotch, and recalled my character's tragic life. It was a lot of lines to learn. To make meaning of the role and remember the lines, I broke down each sentence into beats. For each beat, I had to decide what I was saying and why, what I felt, where I felt it in my body, and where I was in the space. By adding sensory details and motives I got the text into different regions of my brain. I was also creating a map of my emotional/sensory journey onstage which I could attend to in a mindful way.

I remember walking onstage in my long black skirt and white shirt with my hair in a bun. I found my mark

Mindfulness training for actors has led to more spontaneous performances where actors can be present and pay attention to what is happening around them.[6]

by the chair and small table in the dark, then the lights came up. I already had a cigarette lit and was smoking, recounting a memory from Wales.

The playwright Friel was a master craftsman. He created a kind of attention map in his monologues through punctuation cues and changes in emotion and rhythm. It made it easier for me to see, feel, and be in that imagined memory of the Welsh roads. Breaking down the syllables of each word in an Irish brogue brought out the emotions of anger, sadness. It was as if lingering over the syllables in a more sing-song way, and contacting the back of the throat for the brogue, opened up the voice to contain more emotion.

I began my monologue hands shaking, stomach fluttering, but there was a lot to focus on to take me out of fight or flight. After one of the afternoon matinees two ladies approached me, and one had tears in her eyes. "We enjoyed your performance—it was exactly what we needed today."

I added to the map of this great script through my own actions and sensory details—here I would light a cigarette, here I would take a drink of scotch, here I would sit down. Here I was in denial, here I was feeling goosebumps, here I was trying not to cry. All came from a new way of paying attention and retraining my brain in the process.

Paying Attention: What Does It Mean?

Ellen Langer, a professor at Harvard and bestselling author, asked both children and teachers an important research question: "What does it mean when a teacher asks students to pay attention, focus, concentrate on something?"

Most times the answer she got was "to hold that thing still." In other words, she said, "most people think of attention as a kind of mental camera that you keep rigidly, narrowly focused on a particular subject or object." She believes that this is the problem, and when students have trouble paying attention, "they're doing what their teachers say they should do." But it's the wrong instruction.[7] Langer believes, "For us to pay attention to something for any amount of time, the image must be varied."[8] She says, "The most effective way to increase our ability to pay attention is to look for the novelty within the stimulus situation, whether it is a story, a map, or a painting."[9]

Is it that simple? Could focused attention be somehow akin to movement?

At Toluca Lake Elementary School in Los Angeles, students in one second grade class each place a stuffed animal on their bellies and observed the movement of their breath. Afterwards they described it. "Mine was like a dragon," said one student, while another said, "Mine was like smoke."[10]

Teachers at the school noticed a difference in student learning and behavior. "Less conflict on the playground," one said. "Less test anxiety." The children even walked into the classroom in a noticeably different way. The school's state test scores also went up that year, which some of the teachers think had to do with the breathing exercises done right before the test. Even for second graders, mindfulness leads to better attention.

Even for second graders, mindfulness leads to better attention.

The nonprofit organization InnerKids uses this method of mindfulness to train teachers all over the U.S. In a survey done at the Garrison Institute, results of trainings showed that kids were "more responsive and less reactive, more focused and less distracted, more calm and less stressed."[11]

The founder of InnerKids, Susan Kaiser Greenland, says that she tells kids, "mindful awareness is being aware of me, other people, and the world around us."[12]

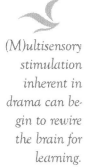

Her description sounds like a great way to pay attention, as well as good tips for acting. The novelty and multisensory stimulation inherent in drama can begin to rewire the brain for learning. "Mindfulness seems to flex the brain circuitry for sustaining attention, an indicator of cognitive control," according to research by Wendy Hasenkamp and Lawrence Barsalou at Emory University.[13]

(M)ultisensory stimulation inherent in drama can begin to rewire the brain for learning.

As we learn more about the neuroscience behind learning and paying attention, we may need these different approaches such as acting or mindfulness to strengthen these neural circuitries so that we can thrive in the classroom.

Chapter 13

Survive and Thrive with the Growth Mindset

In the beginner's mind there are many possibilities,
but in the expert's there are few.
—Shunryo Suzuki, *Zen Mind, Beginner's*
Mind[1]

No matter how expert we may become, we need to continually relearn
how to play with a beginner's bow, beginner's breath, beginner's
body. Thus we recover the innocence, the curiosity, the desire
that impelled us to play in the first place.
—Stephen Nachmonovitch, *Free Play*[2]

The principal at the inner-city elementary school hired me after a
five-minute interview. I was the right person for the job, he said. I
had a pulse. That alone should have caused me concern, but at
the time I had about a hundred dollars in my pocket. My bags
were packed, in my car. If I didn't get a job I was ready to drive
home to move back in with family—not a good solution for a
thirty-year-old adult and retired parents.

The day after the interview, I walked into a bare classroom with
five days to prepare for a class of thirty-six twelve year olds. I'd previ-
ously taught younger kids for short assignments, but I had no idea
what to do with twelve year olds—especially thirty-six of them.

First, I wandered into the school office looking for a friendly face. The principal was bent over his desk. "Put your bulletin boards up, Thérèse," he told me, not looking up. "You need attractive bulletin boards." I shuffled out.

I passed by other rooms where teachers were busy cutting out pictures and patterns for their bulletin boards. I felt like a fraud when I saw the posters of science experiments, multiplication tables, and alphabet letters on the walls. Student names with playful symbols surrounded by fall leaves adorned the classroom doors. I waited for someone to look up, invite me in, but they were trying to meet impossible deadlines, too.

"Don't smile till Thanksgiving," the librarian told me when I went to schedule my class library visits. I thanked her for her generous advice.

By the time I went back to my empty classroom, a feeling of numbness had crept over me. What was I doing here? What was I going to do for six and a half hours each day with thirty-six kids going through puberty? How could I keep them even remotely interested?

As a sixth-grade teacher trained in ESL and German, I would need to learn how to teach math and science too. I had four more days to prep myself on the subject matter.

The week flew by, and many more followed. I got up at 6:00 a.m. to prepare the lesson for each day, grade papers, and make it to school with plenty of time to get the room ready. Recess was always a success because I loved sports. I organized the students into either basketball or jump rope teams, and I joined them in both. But mostly, teaching that year felt like trudging daily through deep thick mud.

There was never enough time in the day to prepare; I couldn't get each period organized and get students to work immediately. We spent a lot of time not knowing exactly what we were working on. I also felt all alone, without any encouragement from staff. No one mentored me or believed in my ability to learn these new skills. I was judged if my students remained silent while in line for the bathroom. This showed the principal whether I was controlling my students or not.

I picked up a few classroom management skills through experimentation. I began to make cooperative learning groups; I organized my room by subject matter. But it wasn't enough to get me to believe in my teaching abilities.

At the end of the year, I walked down to the principal's office, exhausted. "I'm not going to renew my contract next year," I told him.

He was now without a teacher for the fall. He growled back at me, "You'll never make a good teacher anywhere."

I left that office and that school with a heavy heart and stomach.

I had been willing to learn, but this school did not believe in training teachers, giving them enough practice to help them grow their skills, a "growth mindset."

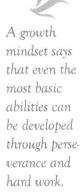

A growth mindset says that even the most basic abilities can be developed through perseverance and hard work.

Over time, I would learn that growth mindset is a clear path to success that doesn't focus on talent but on perseverance. Carol Dweck, a psychologist from Stanford University, first coined the term. "In a fixed mindset," she writes in her book *Mindset*, "people believe their basic qualities, like their intelligence or talent, are simply fixed traits."[3] A growth mindset says that even the most basic abilities can be developed through perseverance and hard work. As Dweck points out, "brains and talent are just the starting point."[4]

My principal in that elementary school used the leadership of fixed mindset. He expected his teachers to just pick up skills, or already have the talent to teach. He did not take feedback well and didn't mentor employees.

Rafe Esquith, the thirty-year veteran teacher from chapter 5 who used Shakespeare with fifth graders, said that most novice teachers with great talent seldom last through the first couple of years without the support of kind mentors.[5] Luckily, in my first three years of teaching college, I found mentors—kind, seasoned professors with growth mindset who nurtured my own talents.

Looking for Growth Mindset

My new mentors told me I could learn the skills to teach even if I didn't have them all from the start. They told me to experiment, that experimentation was a great way to learn.

These mentors breathed life into my teaching, and confidence into me when I had none.

I would often sit down with two of them who taught the same reading course. Our desks were near each other. Because there weren't any high cubicle walls, you could stand up and find anyone you were looking for. Around and around we would go exploring books, strategies, possibilities. It was with their encouragement that I began to experiment with drama. Going to work suddenly was a joy and felt safe. We were all growing together as teachers. These mentors breathed life into my teaching, and confidence into me when I had none. I wasn't a great teacher when I started; how could I be? But there was something I loved about it, and I wasn't afraid to work hard at improving my skills. That's growth mindset at work.

Not all my colleagues at the college shared my curiosity and need for experimenting with the curriculum.

122

I remember one meeting where several of us gathered in a white-walled room. We were equals: we all had similar degrees, all taught the same course, and most of us loved what we did. But the two of us assigned to design the course had only been teaching for about three years compared to the seasoned veterans. We loved the course because we could experiment with books we were passionate about.

We began to explain our choices in the small conference room. Immediately there were objections.

"What about a textbook? How are you going to measure what students learn? And how are you going to teach the skills they need at this level?"

"We are going to teach those skills within the framework of our chosen books," I stammered, sweaty palms suddenly. Teachers looked at me, waiting for a more intelligent response.

"Do you have those ready?"

"Some, not all." My co-designer sat rigid and still. One of the seasoned teachers looked at us and proclaimed, "You two don't seem to know what you're doing with the curriculum."

My chest caved in. The words entered my body with force. I looked over at my co-designer—his face was red, his eyes were glued to our agenda. This professor had hit us where it hurt, in our heartfelt teaching methods that we had agonized over for days. I didn't have the skills I needed to lob a pedagogical point back at her, so I sat silent, not sure how to respond to such a fixed mindset.

Rafe Esquith explains people with the fixed mindset as those "teachers you need to avoid.... These negative folks do not thrive in solitary confinement, and they invite discouraged young teachers to join their circle of misery. I urge you to stay away from them."[6] The professor's biting remark stayed with me a long time. But it also stretched me. I had to adopt one of

123

the tenets of growth mindset, to not let criticism of my work diminish me.

Critics are the dumbbells to our creativity muscles. The more we can exorcise them out of our minds, the more we can exercise our own patience, determination, and teaching skills, and take our next step. Within a few more years, I developed the ability to keep going despite obstacles like the pain of failure and personalized criticism.

Grit: An Important Piece of the Puzzle

Angela Duckworth is a psychologist who studied grit in Chicago public schools. She found that grit was the most important quality to student success. She defines it as "the tendency to sustain interest in and effort toward long term goals."[7]

Grittier kids were more likely to graduate. Grit was more important than whether or not a kid felt safe at school, was financially secure, or had a higher IQ.

"Talent doesn't make you gritty," Duckworth said. In fact, grit is unrelated or even inversely related to talent.

How do you build grit? According to Duckworth, you teach kids about growth mindset. When kids read and learn about the brain and learn how the brain responds and grows to challenge, they are more likely to persevere when they fail because they don't see failure as a permanent condition.

Brain activity is different for fixed mindset and growth mindset people. For those with a fixed mindset, brain scans show that brain activity increases when they are praised for results or a grade. People with a growth mindset show the most brain activity and paid more attention when praised for their hard work and effort.

(Grit is) "the tendency to sustain interest in and effort toward long term goals."[7]

They are not as concerned with being judged. And again, when growth mindset people fail, they don't see it as a permanent state. But when people with a fixed mindset fail, they lose interest or withdraw.[8]

From a growth mindset, I realized I didn't have to know every classroom situation and how to teach through it. I could keep going, keep trying. Eventually a solution would present itself.

Teach Growth Mindset and Grit Follows

Inez, from Colombia brought in two pieces of writing done for one of my classes. One was a single paragraph, which she had started in class and finished at home. The other was a book report which I had assigned for homework. I looked at both. The first was full of grammar mistakes; however, I could see how she tried to link independent phrases and ideas together and express herself in a complex fashion.

The second piece of writing was perfect, completed by someone who was a native speaker. She had read the book, she told me, but she had received help with writing the book report.

I went back to her single paragraph. "You see this sentence here," I pointed. "You've got a great idea that you develop with your next sentence. Sure, you have to work on agreement, but so do most students in this class."

She blushed.

I added, "I want more of this; make more mistakes like this!"

"Really?" She let out a sigh. "I know I can do that." We both smiled.

It felt like a fog lifted. After that talk, Inez brought in many writing assignments for me to check. She seemed less fearful of the teacher's red pen, more interested in practice. She didn't cringe when she handed in writing assignments but was willing to try to complete each assignment. She even asked me for extra assignments. By the end of the semester, she was writing more developed paragraphs on her own.

Inez had started the semester at the bottom of the class, but she finished in the top half. Permission to grow and learn, to make mistakes, made all the difference.

We do this not by praising their intelligence but by praising their effort. This helps develop grit.[9]

In an interview in *Education World*, Carol Dweck shares that the greatest gift we can give our students is to show them how to thrive on obstacles and to love learning. We do this not by praising their intelligence but by praising their effort. This helps develop grit.

Students who succeed in learning a new skill, like language, can withstand the frustration of putting their ideas together without knowing if they will be correct. To adapt a growth mindset you need to focus on questions like: What did I learn today? What mistake did I make that taught me something? What did I try hard at today?

"It is impossible to tell what people are capable of," says Dweck, "...if they catch fire and apply themselves."[9]

Barriers to Growth Mindset

Entering my sixteenth year of teaching, I was an "expert" according to *Outliers'* author Malcolm Gladwell.[10] I had my 10,000 hours of experience, yet I was struggling, trying out Shakespeare scenes with beginning language students for the first time. After two weeks of practice, I began to doubt my choices. Did they really need to know words like *doth* and *thou*? I had never tried Shakespeare scenes with beginning classes, and it wasn't easy. The voice of doubt was louder than the voice of growth mindset.

126

"I'll never memorize this," Miguel said during rehearsal. "You're not going to make us memorize it, are you?"

"What does this mean here?" asked his girlfriend Miriam. "Do I need to say this?"

Every semester I faced this kind of doubt to some degree. I would wonder: Should I stick with the textbook only and not add dramatic scripts? Even though it was always fun, and the potential for student transformation was great, I struggled with giving myself permission for such an experiment. Then I'd remind myself that this same doubt occurred almost every other time I tried something new in the classroom. So I just kept going.

Miguel had been an architect in Colombia but had put his career on hold when he came to the US. I found out later that he had suffered a brain injury from a fall, which wiped out his ability to quickly absorb certain content, like grammar. But he had elected to play Richard III. Miriam played Queen Elizabeth.

The weeks before our performance were a nightmare. Miguel spent most of the class gossiping with Miriam or sneaking texts on his cell phone. But the day of the play, he changed. He stood proud in front of the class with Miriam poised three feet away, and his voice came out booming, perfectly articulate: "Stay, madam; I must speak a word with you." I looked at the students around me. Their gaping mouths told me they too were surprised. We all knew Miguel.

"I have no more sons of the royal blood for thee to murder," replied a bitter Queen Elizabeth.

Miguel responded loud and clear in Richard III's voice: "You have a daughter call'd Elizabeth, virtuous and fair, royal and gracious."

Later, before he left that night, I stopped him on his way out of class, "Miguel, that was an incredible Richard III."

"Thanks." A grin lit up across his face. "It was fun."

"Had you performed Shakespeare before this?" I stepped aside to let the last student pass by.

"No." He looked me in the eye. "I used to stand up and talk in front of clients all the time in Colombia." He looked down biting his lip. "But it's been a while."

Somehow Miguel had remembered this and tapped into the growth mindset. And I learned that class didn't need to be perfect. That was fixed mindset thinking. I just had to keep experimenting to provide opportunities for my students, and stretch myself so that each day would be new. It was good to feel like a beginner.

... class didn't need to be perfect. That was fixed mindset thinking.

Doubt: A Healthy Attitude

Richard Feynman, a Nobel Prize recipient for his work in quantum electrodynamics, was never certain. Feynman believed that an attitude of doubt opened the channel for new inventions.[11]

Sir Andre Geim is a Russian-born scientist who won the 2010 Nobel Prize, along with Konstantin Novoselov, for their work on graphene, one of the strongest materials known. Graphene conducts heat better than diamond, and may conduct electricity better than silver. Geim and Novoselov discovered the uses of graphene in the lab during their "Friday evening experiments."

"We devote 10 percent of our time to so-called 'Friday evening' experiments," said Novoselov. "I just do all kinds of crazy things that probably won't pan out at all, but if they do, it would be really surprising." Geim even tried frog levitation as one of his experiments. "There are many more that were unsuccessful and never went anywhere...[but] I love them no less than the successful ones."[12]

Doubt or uncertainty gives us the space to discover; in this space, we can relax. It is the opposite of vying for power to control others with a point of view.

With this open approach, Novoselov noticed "a stream of coincidences that basically brought us some very remarkable results."[13]

CHAPTER 14

It Takes Guts

This being human is a guest house.
Every morning a new arrival.
A joy, a depression, a meanness,
some momentary awareness comes
as an unexpected visitor.
Welcome and entertain them all! . . .
The dark thought, the shame, the malice,
meet them at the door laughing,
and invite them in.
Be grateful for whatever comes,
because each has been sent
as a guide from beyond.
> —Rumi, "The Guest House,"
> translated by Coleman Barks[1]

"*Listen to your gut. You'll know what to do.*"
"*Follow your heart, it knows.*"

These pearls of wisdom appealed to me during turning points in my life, but for a long time my gut was too tangled up in knots for me to hear its wisdom.

By the time I was twelve, my gut was in trouble. My parents had irreconcilable differences, and life was chaotic. When my father came home from work, we kids would flock to him for hugs, but my mother's steely silent gaze never left her work at the kitchen stove.

We sat down to dinner, and my three brothers filled the silence with *Monty Python* and *Blazing Saddles* reenactments. My mother laughed sporadically at her sons' jokes, between sips of her chianti. By high school, the polarity between my parents was dramatic. While one volunteered for Planned Parenthood, the other picketed against abortion outside. At night I watched, heart sad, as my father played solitaire and listened to Roger Miller songs, while my mother walked stiffly around the house, sending critical remarks toward me and sharing silence with the rest of the family.

I learned to tune out my gut, because it was screaming. I didn't want to hear its pained rumblings.

I learned to tune out my gut, because it was screaming. I didn't want to hear its pained rumblings.

Focusing: Listening to the Body

Eugene Gendlin, recipient of four awards from the American Psychological Association, published important research focusing on why some patients benefited from psychotherapy and some did not.

Clients who did well in therapy "seemed willing to deal with unclear aspects of their experience," Gendlin said. "They were listening to or sensing some totality of their inner experience that was vague.... As the client 'focused' on this vague sensation, giving it attention and respect, the inner experience became clearer and a space opened up for new insights and unexpected possibilities. The 'felt sense' of the situation changed and the change felt good. The shift in their bodily-felt experience often led to changes in behavior."[2]

I learned this method, called "Focusing," after sur-
viving a number of challenging relationships. Focusing
asked me to listen with neutral, careful attention to mind
and body. I had already become more aware of thoughts,
emotions, and physical sensations through voice work
and acting, but the focusing work I did for three years
was transformational.

Recently, after a stressful situation with a friend
where I was afraid I had been too blunt, I felt great unease in my body. I decided to try focusing.

It was late morning; I had just finished my tea, and
the birds had finished chirping. I went to the sofa and
sat with my feet crossed underneath me. I focused first
on my body: how my back felt supported, how my legs
felt on the sofa. I watched the rise and fall of my chest as
I took some breaths.

Then I asked my body where there was an issue.
My attention went to my stomach: lots of butterflies. I
tried to find the exact word to describe the feeling. It
felt fluttery, panicky. There was heat, terror. I settled
on a "fluttery heat." When I called it fluttery heat, I
noticed I relaxed a little. The words opened up space
in my body—aligning correct words with correct feeling. I spent a little more time sensing what was going
on, asking my stomach if there was anything else it
wanted to tell me.

Then my attention went to a pain in my jaw.

I observed the jaw as tight, hard, painful, sore. It felt
cranky and worn out—like it was locked up for a long time.
As soon as I noticed this, I decided to ask this part of myself,
"What do you want?" I listened to some reasons my jaw gave
me as to why it felt locked up.

*Focusing
asked me
to listen
with neutral,
careful
attention to
mind and
body.*

By noticing these sensations and naming them, more space opened up. And soon the tension was gone. I knew this tension in my jaw was from being afraid to speak up as a child. When I did tell someone the truth, as I had with my friend, the same sensations came up in my body.

I didn't solve all my problems in that focusing session, but most of my stress was gone by the end of it, and it allowed me to look at the problem in a fresh way.

Ann Weiser Cornell, a student of Gendlin's, writes that when we allow ourselves to feel the sensations in our body without letting them take over (for example, "I notice anger" or "I notice stiffness," as opposed to "I am angry" or "I am stiff"), we can learn from these sensations. "Our bodies carry knowledge about how we are living our lives," Cornell says, "about what we need to be more fully ourselves, about what we value and believe, about what has hurt us emotionally and how to heal it."[3]

"Our bodies carry knowledge about how we are living our lives."[3]

Although Gendlin cautions against a rigid set of steps, he offers them as a starting point for anyone who wants to practice the technique. The following is adapted from his book *Focusing* and appears on the Focusing Institute's website.[4]

1. Clearing a Space: Just relax and ask, "How is my life going? What is the main thing for me now?" Sense within your body. Let the answers come slowly from this sensing. When some concern comes, *do not go inside it.* Stand back, say "Yes, that's there. I can feel that there." Let there be a little

space between you and that. Then ask what else you feel. Wait again, and sense. Usually there are several things.

2. Felt Sense: From among what came, select one personal problem to focus on. *Do not go inside it.* Stand back from it. Of course, there are many parts to that one thing you are thinking about—too many to think of each one alone. But you can *feel* all of these things together. Pay attention where you usually feel things, and in there you can get a sense of what all of the problem feels like.

3. Handle: What is the quality of this unclear felt sense? Let a word, a phrase, or an image come up from the felt sense itself. It might be a word like *tight, sticky, scary, stuck, heavy, jumpy,* or a phrase, or an image. Stay with the quality of the felt sense till something fits it just right.

4. Resonating: Go back and forth between the felt sense and the word, phrase, or image. Check how they resonate with each other. See if there is a little bodily signal that lets you know there is a fit. To do that, you have to have the felt sense there again, as well as the word. Let the felt sense change, if it does, and also the word or picture, until they feel just right.

5. Asking: Now ask, what is it about this whole problem that makes this quality (what you have just named or pictured)? Make sure the quality is sensed again, freshly, vividly (not just remembered from before). When it is here again, tap it, touch it, be with it, asking, "What makes the whole problem so _____?" Or ask, "What is in *this* sense?"

If you get a quick answer without a shift in the felt

sense, just let that kind of answer go by. Return your attention to your body and freshly find the felt sense again. Then ask it again.

Be with the felt sense till something comes along with a shift, a slight "give" or release.

6. Receiving: Receive whatever comes with a shift in a friendly way. Stay with it a while, even if it is only a slight release. Whatever comes, this is only one shift; there will be others. You will probably continue after a little while, but stay here for a few moments.

If you have spent a little while sensing and touching an unclear, holistic body sense of this problem, then you have focused. It doesn't matter whether the body-shift came or not. It comes on its own. We don't control that.

Used by permission.

Clearing Blocks

Blockages or resistance, my words for "fear," used to prevent me from taking action. For example, it was difficult to sit down and write this chapter. Having to put into words the anxiety I didn't even want to acknowledge for many years brought familiar physical unease to my chest and gut. I worried how it would be received. Getting close to criticism on issues so dear to me brought up even more childhood angst. For a while I was stuck. I distracted myself with cleaning and eating. I put the task off for many weeks. In fact, I went to delete the whole chapter one morning but found a comment from a reader, "This was some of my favorite information."

"Oh, God," I sighed as I read the comment. I went to the kitchen to eat something. I scrounged the refrigerator and found some cottage cheese and an apple.

I finished eating and sat back down on the couch. Okay, I thought. I can do focusing right now, then write about it.

I got quiet. I listened to the disturbance in my gut. I wrote to it. I tried to identify the image or sense word connected to the feeling. It took me a while, but I came up with words to describe the feeling—dark cloud, terror, abandoned. When I hit on the sensing image that felt right, I noticed that wonderful shift in my body. Nauseousness passed, tightening released.

I listened to the disturbance in my gut. I wrote to it.

I eventually worked through enough blocks for me to go back to my writing. Focusing helped me work through the block and take action.

Gut: Our Second Brain

When I was young, it was difficult to make "gut" decisions. I also had trouble with follow through and finishing. Once I got started on something, familiar fearful thoughts would creep in: What if I fail? What if I succeed? I didn't know how to tune into any wisdom in the gut, the second brain for many of us.

Michael Gershon, MD, coined the phrase "second brain."[5] The enteric nervous system, which governs the gastrointestinal system, has 100 million neurons and can function on its own. It contains thirty different neurotransmitters. Of these, it harbors 90 percent of the serotonin in the body and 50 percent of the body's dopamine. It carries signals up to the brain and from the brain to the enteric nervous system through the vagus nerve. Most of the communication of the vagus nerve is upward—from gut brain to head brain. The field of enteric science studies the microbiome of the gut and how it affects the brain and overall health.

Focusing is a way to tap into this second brain. It's a way other than talk therapy to get students out of a difficult situation in class. When they are panicked or stressed, I bring their focus gently to their body sensations. Together with movement, drama, and group support, focusing has been very successful in helping students bypass panic and take action in rehearsals.

The Power of Lady Bracknell Revisited

A week before classes began one semester, a Russian man and his son came by my desk at the college. He asked if he could sign up his wife for my speech class. I asked him where his wife was.

"She's too anxious to come to school," he replied.

I straightened in my chair. "Does she know this is an oral communication class?"

"Oh, yes," he said, and went to register her.

Two weeks into the semester, I asked for volunteers to play various parts in about ten different scenes. Almost every semester, I use scenes from Oscar Wilde's *The Importance of Being Earnest*. I mentioned this play in chapter 4, when Anh used movement to transform her performance. I rely on such well-carved characters, like Oscar Wilde's Lady Bracknell and Marsha Norman's Jessie and Thelma in *'night Mother*, over and over in my teaching. My shy Russian student, Viktoria, who had not opened her mouth except when I asked her a question directly, volunteered to play Lady Bracknell.

The first few weeks, Viktoria's voice was soft, difficult to hear. She stood with slouching shoulders, terribly miscast for this role of an eloquent, upper-crust British matron. Early on, at one rehearsal, Viktoria pulled me aside. "I don't think I want to rehearse today," she said.

"What's going on?" I asked her. Students were assembling into groups in the classroom, waiting to begin.

"I don't feel well. My stomach." Viktoria looked down at the floor.

"What's it feel like?"

"Cramped. I think I'm sick." The groups were beginning to move chairs.

"Can you take some deep breaths?" I began to demonstrate.

She nodded, started breathing.

"It happens. Let's just walk through the rehearsal with your notes." I watched her to see if she was going to move toward the rehearsal space in front of the room.

After a few deep breaths, Viktoria picked up her notes.

Rather than talk her out of being nervous, which doesn't work so well, I added, "Just notice the feeling, Viktoria, and let it be."

Rehearsals went more easily. I reminded Viktoria to breathe when I saw her tensing up. For final performance day, she wore a large hat with flowers wrapped around the brim and a long skirt. She walked on stage, shoulders back, chin up, lips pressed tight together. A perfect Lady Bracknell.

With pen in hand ready to keep score on her interviewee's answers, she asked her scene partner, "I have always been of opinion that a man who desires to get married should know either everything or nothing. Which do you know?"

I always like to watch the audience to see if they're enjoying the play. Twenty classmates and three visitors looked on, many capturing the performance on their iPhones. The two players finished, bowed, and loped off the stage, smiling.

"That was fantastic," I told Viktoria later. "You weren't nervous?"

She looked up with me with her big brown eyes, and in a resonant voice announced, "I'm not afraid of anything after Lady Bracknell."

In Afghanistan, focusing is used by therapists to help people with PTSD. The Sufi poet Rumi, himself born in Afghanistan, hints at the modern practice of focusing in his poem "The Guesthouse." Focusing therapy is comforting to Afghans. "Because Afghans seem to have a head start on focusing, we describe it to Afghans as being a simple way of paying attention to the insides of ourselves, the place of wisdom, and the places that hurt," said one therapist.[6]

Scientists and medical doctors have termed the communication between gut and brain the "gut-brain axis."[7] New discoveries show that when the brain is not functioning properly, symptoms often exist in the gut, and vice versa. This gut-brain axis is dependent on many factors: healthy functioning of the vagus nerve, healthy gut flora (microbiome), and healthy emotions. Stress can negatively affect the balance of flora in the gut, and a stressful early childhood has been linked to life-long compromises in the gut–brain axis.

Many unresolved questions, though, are still being researched: How exactly does gut flora—this microbiome of living organisms—influence and communicate with our brain? How does stress affect the gut–brain axis over time? What can we do to reverse this situation?

As I began to listen to my gut, acknowledge the emotions and sensations there, my stress decreased and my overall health improved. I made physical improvements such as practicing qigong and making dietary changes, but tuning into the emotions and senses through focusing was very powerful.

CHAPTER 15

Peaceful Warrior Teacher

*I call myself a warrior—a peaceful warrior—
because the real battles we face are inside us.*
—Dan Millman,
Way of the Peaceful Warrior[1]

It was Halloween night as I walked to class. Darkness competed with the moon that peeked out through the clouds. I arrived in the empty classroom and put my books and notebook on my desk, as always, scanning the quiet room for order and peace. I felt none. I didn't trust myself with this group of students: my voice often sounded hesitant as it drifted out to them; my feet felt wobbly as I stood in front of them. It seemed like there was a curse on every activity I tried. I'd tried everything I've shared in these chapters, with little success.

I waited for ghouls to howl.

Outside the classroom window, students passed by in their costumes. Makeup and dark circles were painted around their eyes, hair was dyed purple. It completely mirrored my despair. I waited for ghouls to howl.

I returned my glance to the empty class and glared at my textbook. I didn't like the text. Explanations were missing, leaving both me and my students confused.

141

Tests supplied by the book were more difficult than any exercises given.

Students filed in late that night, and I pressed forward with my usual smile: "Hello and welcome." One student slammed his books on his desk and muttered, "Yeah, it's a good night—except that we have to be here!" I winced.

An eerie feeling rolled over the class. Angry glares from normally calm students roamed around the room, focused on me. I heard the the branches of the trees hit the windows as the wind blew through them. What's going on? I wondered, trying to ignore both my gut and chest.

Finally class was over. I said goodbye and slumped into my chair to put my things back in my bag for the night.

One student remained, hunched over, eyes searching me out, wanting to talk. Amy, from Peru. "Teacher," she faltered, swallowing some intense emotion trying to surface.

"Yes, Amy, what is it?"

"I'm having trouble in this class." Now her sighs were audible. She couldn't push her anxiety down any further. Sobs erupted.

"What is it, Amy? How can I help?"

Amy wiped at the tears as they fell quickly from her eyes. "These students don't like you. They are *pendejos*. They say one thing to your face and another to each other."

My heart hurt from the words. "They don't like me, really?" I asked—for a moment more interested in my own welfare than poor Amy's shaking body.

She shook her head. I let go of my own hurt and focused again on her.

"Amy, I think you are doing great in this class. Your writing is coming along. It's wonderful having you in class, you add so much."

"Thank you, teacher. You are so organized and explain things so well. You are a good teacher. They are just stupid."

I thanked her for her comments, and we discussed her next steps with a counselor to help her deal with her anxiety. But I walked to my car in a stupor. I was worried about Amy, yes, but she would be all right, now that she had identified she needed help. I could follow up with her throughout the semester with help from counseling.

... the shock that these students didn't respect me scraped at my insides.

But the shock that these students didn't respect me scraped at my insides. As ugly as their behavior was, preying on my vulnerability when all I was doing was everything in my power to teach them, I saw there was an important lesson to face.

From Wimp to Warrior

At home, my husband and our dog sat on the couch, watching *Jeopardy*. My husband turned when I came in. "What is it?" he said. I put my hands to my heart. "Help!" I shut off the TV.

I told him what had happened. He got up and went to the bookshelf, pulling out a book of inspirational quotes and exercises.

"You've got to imagine something different for yourself," he said. "I bet there's something helpful in here." He handed me the book.

We sat down and together devised a few creative exercises using imaginative techniques. Becoming aware of what was going on in the class had been my impetus to change. Now I had four days of a long weekend to step into the new and necessary awareness to handle it.

Over the weekend, I first practiced using a different speaking voice—one that was unapologetic, firm—as I shared in chapters 2 and 3. I felt more sure of myself, more grounded, when I lowered my voice and used chest resonance.

Next, I wrote about my fears and insecurities, meditated, and contemplated. I did more qigong, and I used Emotional Freedom Techniques, or "tapping." EFT is a therapy system where you physically tap on acupressure points on your head, face, and sternum while describing first the emotional problem then a new solution. I had spent months learning the tapping technique. With practice, I began to feel a shift, as if habitual negative thoughts and emotional patterns were breaking up.

Dr. Gary Craig is the founder of EFT, or Emotional Freedom Technique. He has described this technique as follows:

"EFT stands for Emotional Freedom Techniques (sometimes called tapping) and, in essence, it is an emotional version of acupuncture, except we don't use needles. Instead, we stimulate certain meridian points on the body by tapping on them with our fingertips.

"The cause of all negative emotions is a disruption in the body's energy system.

"It follows, then, that energy disruptions are the reason we have any kind of emotional issue like grief, anger, guilt, depression, trauma, or fear. Since both physical and performance issues often have emotional roots, it also follows that clearing energy disruptions can be useful for those as well.

"Once we find those energy disruptions, we use the tapping process to correct them. The EFT Tapping Basic Recipe blends focused wording with a nine-point tapping sequence. The focused wording tunes us into the issue and this, in turn, points us to the energy disruptions that we need to address.

"This wording is an essential part of the process because it tells our system what we are working on. Negative emotions come about because we are tuned into certain thoughts or circumstances which, in turn, cause our energy systems to disrupt. Otherwise, we function normally. One's fear of heights is not present, for example, while one is reading the comic section of the Sunday newspaper (and therefore not tuned into the problem).

"Once tuned into the issue, the tapping stimulates the energy pathways thereby balancing the resulting energy disruptions.

"This innovative tapping tool has proven useful in clinical settings for just about any emotional, physical, or performance issue you can name." [2]

Used by permission.

Working with Brad Yates in a phone session,[3] I identified strong emotions, rated them between 1-10, then tapped on the acupressure points on my head, face, and sternum. In the case of my difficult class, I tapped with my finger tips on the points, voiced the phrase "I feel anxious about my class," then eventually tapped "I let go of the anxiety around my class." I noticed immediate relief.

At several points over the four-day weekend, as I spent time in contemplation, I saw myself as a giant container of light. Light was pouring around me, and through my head, down my body, out my legs and tailbone. I wasn't "pumping myself up" to feel good, but was trying to see myself as a source of joy and love. Granted, I had been working on things like this for years off and on, but now I was under the gun. I had to replace the "I need people to like me" syndrome.

The night before my return to class, I thought of one last thing to do. I took out some red nail polish, sat on my balcony, and painted my toenails and fingernails like a warrior preparing for battle; this tiny change helped me feel even more of a shift.

As I faced the class the next evening, I felt the solidness of my feet planted firmly on the ground. The cotton of my shirt and pants molded naturally to my skin. When I stood at the board, I wrote with more ease, taking deep breaths. As I spoke, my newly solid voice coursed through me into the room with resonance, a lower tone, a strength that hadn't been there before.

That evening, to my surprise, the students returned from break exactly on time. They sat quietly in their seats and looked at me with wide eyes, pens ready to write. There was no snickering—only quiet study and focused discussion as they moved into group work.

Once or twice they tested me to see if this change was real. "I want to talk to you about my grades!" one student interrupted.

"You can make an appointment with me after class," I shot back without missing a beat. No negativity entered me—neither a need to control nor a need to react. I was neutral.

I drove home that night feeling like the peaceful warrior teacher. Being a peaceful warrior inside helped me change my

146

internal dialogue, subdue my fear, and feel confident but detached. My strength came from knowing exactly what I wanted to accomplish in class. I had nothing left to prove, and my identity was no longer tied to a need to be liked.

Being a peaceful warrior inside helped me change my internal dialogue

With this clear viewpoint, I began to see what my students really needed. They struggled with the obscure textbook explanations, so I added more examples and more review. Later in the week I gave them a practice test before the real chapter test, so they could more easily succeed.

The new attitude, the new voice, worked. My new teaching strategies worked. The students got more reflection time, more time to assimilate material in more ways.

My "four-day turn around" had been in the works for many years. By the end of class, several weeks later, three students came up and thanked me. As I walked home in the crisp December, I realized that by giving up the need for approval, I now had it.

As Dan Millman, author of *The Way of the Peaceful Warrior*, writes, "When you begin your transcendental training, focusing your best efforts, without attachment to outcomes, you will understand the peaceful warrior's way."[4]

Teaching is an art and a science. The training and skills you get from your subject matter and degree count. But the art is what happens in the moment, how you react, and what you create with others.

Chapter 16

Say Yes to Improv(e) Your Life

In the movie Yes Man, *Jim Carey agrees to say yes to opportunities in his life at the urgings of a self-help guru,* and his life transforms from predictable and boring to passionate. He finds true love with a quirky photographer, stops an attempted suicide, and learns a new language. I left the theater wondering what I could say yes to, to add more joy to my own life.

Not long after, I auditioned for an improvisational comedy group. I wanted to take more chances and thought improv comedy would help me do this. Despite years of helping students with anxiety via classroom plays, I was still anxious about performing myself. I also missed the challenge and thrill of live theater.

In improv comedy, you create skits and stories right in the moment from structured games. I made it through the audition and practiced improv for several months with the troupe, ending up with a new attitude about the power of yes.

It began with an improvisation I created with two other ensemble members.

We set a chair in the center of the stage. The rule was that the person on the chair had to say his line and then move off the chair for the next person to say his. We had to listen to what was said, accept what was offered from our scene partner, and build on it.

Our coach gave us an imagined setting: We were at a family funeral. The rest we had to invent as we went along.

I stood, waiting for my turn at the chair, adrenaline running through me.

I stood, waiting for my turn at the chair, adrenaline running through me. My partner, Ray, sat down.

"I miss him already. Great man." And rising from the chair, he added, "I'm going to get a drink."

I sat down on the chair, imagining the funeral. "Get me one, too. He looks good—I think that's Armani." I couldn't think of anything else to say, so I hopped off the chair so Sheila, the third partner, could add to the dialogue. She started to lean to the side, tipsy from alcohol.

By the time I reached the chair the third or fourth time, the story had evolved: I knew that we were at the funeral of my deceased relative, I was in an unhappy marriage, and I was drinking to escape the pain. Our coach clapped, our signal to finish the skit. I jumped back to my seat off the stage, satisfied. I'd said yes to each line my improv partners offered, and the story grew in surprising ways.

One member of our group, who didn't last long performing with us, was a heavyset man in the film business. Whenever I was onstage with him, I knew he was thinking about his next clever funny remark. His remark might be funny, but it came out of the past, a preplanned idea that wasn't a yes response to what anyone else had said. We were never connected, and it made it impossible to create something new. The skits always fell flat.

The rest of the crew went on to perform in local venues, but I dropped out after a while. I stopped in to see them perform whenever I was free. One time they called me up onstage for a skit. My heart was pounding loud and heavy, and it felt like it would leap out of my throat, but I just reminded myself to listen, say yes inside. To my surprise and relief, the skit was both fun and funny.

As frightening as improv was, the principles of saying yes contain a few secrets to freedom and success: I *had* to listen to others; by listening to others, I could escape some of my self-consciousness and create something new. When we all said yes, I gained confidence because I knew others were really listening and responding to what I said. My brain functioned better, I felt. And by failing in front of people in a skit, I learned to fear failure less.

(A)ctors "learn how to fail, because you mostly flop. You learn to not be afraid to fail....[1]

In an interview, Tina Fey explained that actors "learn how to fail, because you mostly flop. You learn to not be afraid to fail.... You also learn to support other actors on stage." She spoke admiringly of the famous Second City Theater: "You can put Second City people in a scene and they'll make the other people look good as opposed to trying to show off themselves."[1] Saying yes is a partnership of listening. "With improvisation," she said, "all you're supposed to be doing is putting all your attention on your partner and listening to everything they're saying, and it takes you out of watching yourself because you can't."[2]

Here are my favorite improv rules. I use them in life and the classroom, to teach myself and my students the power of saying yes.

Accept what is offered.

Say "yes, and" as opposed to "yes, but."

There are no mistakes, only opportunities.

Give and take: even when you're talking, be listening, and if someone else starts to talk, stop talking.

151

Keith Johnstone is an internationally known teacher of improv. Here is a sample of a scene from a Keith Johnstone class. This first section shows what happens when actors break the "say yes" rules and don't accept what their partners offer.

A: *I'm having trouble with my leg.*
B: *I'm afraid I'll have to amputate.*
A: *You can't do that, Doctor. Because I'm rather attached to it.*
B: (Losing heart) *Come on, man.*[3]

The joke above got laughs, but the scene went nowhere. Person A negated the offer with "You can't do that, Doctor." Then person B didn't have any options, had to ask "Why not?" and the scene died. In this next example, the story takes on a new life because each person accepts the offer given.

A: *Augh!*
B. *Whatever is it, man?*
A: *It's my leg, Doctor.*
B: *This looks nasty. I shall have to amputate.*
A: *It's the one you amputated last time, Doctor.*
B: *You mean you've got a pain in your wooden leg?*
A: *Yes, Doctor.*
B: *You know what this means!*
A: *Woodworm, Doctor!*
B: *Yes. We'll have to remove it before it spreads to the rest of you.* (A's chair collapses)
B: *My God! It's spreading to the furniture!*[4]

Charles Limb, MD, researched the effects of improv on the brain, observing jazz musicians and rappers under the fMRI scanner. He saw more activity in various regions of the brain when they improvised compared to when they played memorized material. Also, while improvising, the musicians' brains lit up in the self-expressive area of the brain (medial prefrontal) while other areas of the brain which controlled self-censorship were not activated (lateral prefrontal). Limb concluded that "to be creative you have to have this weird disassociation in your frontal lobe. One area turns on and another area shuts off so you're not inhibited. So you're willing to make mistakes."[5]

I gave a teacher training at a conference for Florida colleges on "Practicing Dramatic Techniques to Overcome Anxiety and Accelerate Learning." It was a busy part of the teaching semester, and both faculty and staff were tired. They entered the room silently, slumped in their chairs, taking a moment to finish their breakfasts of scones and coffee. A group of staff members who knew each other congregated in the middle. Up front, sat men and women in two-piece suits. A lone faculty member sat over on the left side, his glasses low on the ridge of his nose. I couldn't even tell if his eyes were open.

I got them up right away, just as I do my college students. We started with qigong breathing and shoulder shrugs. Eyes widened, bodies seemed more energized, so I broke them into small groups of four or five, telling them about the rules of improvisation and the "safe approach to learning," as I had started to call this attitude of saying yes.

We moved the desks back to make an open space for their circles, then we began.

First was a simple counting exercise. Circle exercises are typical warm-ups in improv classes. They help you think on your feet, listen to what comes before you. Next, I asked them to create a sentence in their circle. Finally, I asked them to create a story beginning with "Once upon a time...," still going round their little group. I began to hear some giggling as voices got louder.

They stood tall and alert when we started the final exercise. For this, they worked in groups of two. I put dialogue up on the screen for all to see:

Person A: *It's been such a long time since we've seen each other.*
Person B: *I know. Time really does fly.*
Person A: *So much has changed since that day.*
Person B: *I know just what you mean.*
Person A: *Do you remember the last thing we said to each other?*
Person B: *It's hard to forget. In fact, I don't think I'll ever forget.*

Each pair was to pick an imaginary scenario—were they two brothers, long lost friends, colleagues at work? Then they decided the subtext, or underlying meaning, of the dialogue. After practicing for a few minutes, I asked for pairs of volunteers to share their skits. The rest of us had to guess the scenario: who they were, where they were, and why they were meeting. Almost every group volunteered to share their skit.

Two women, who had been giggling as they practiced, delivered their dialogue with loud voices, one upset and one sheepish, gesturing and pointing fingers at each other. We guessed they were long-lost friends who'd had a fight. We clapped, and another group shared their skit.

At the end of the workshop, I asked the faculty what they would take back to their classrooms to use with their students. "I'm an administrator," one man said. "I can see using the principle of 'yes, and' instead of the 'yes, but' at my meetings to get people to share or encourage ideas." A woman added, "It was a great warm-up for the brain—I would use it to get students more involved and wake them up."

As I filed out of the the room after them, they walked with lighter feet, talking to each other. In only forty-five minutes, saying yes had shifted the energy of a whole room.

Improv Comedy at the Large Hadron Collider

Improv and saying yes are not only useful in schools. In Geneva resides the world's largest particle accelerator, managed by CERN (known as European Organization for Nuclear Research). Physicists and scientists use CERN to research black holes and other dimensions. In 2008, the staff at the research center was under serious scrutiny from the public: Could their experiments with the Large Hadron Collider create a black hole?

To improve communication among staff and the concerned public, one of the physicists at CERN, Bob Stanek, did something quite radical. He hired an improv comedy coach from Chicago to work with the scientists.

In an interview with NPR's Jacki Lyden, Stanek explained why he brought in Charna Halpern to teach improv. "It shows physicists that they need to think out of the box," Stanek said. He thought that improv could help them get rid of this "negative attitude that most physicists tend to have." It would train them to say yes.[6]

CHAPTER 17

The "Safe" Approach to Learning Language

Language learning is also improvisation. Learners need to use many areas of the brain to listen and make language. If it's a new language, this requires making new synapses.

The rules of improv help us access more creativity-where creative ideas come "out of nowhere."

I wanted to provide such a creative climate for my students, where they could learn to listen actively, experiment, and feel accepted. Over years of testing and development, I began to call my strategy the "safe approach to learning," and it became useful in many areas of my teaching career.

I began to call my strategy the "safe approach to learning...."

I remember one student in particular, Kamal. A recent transplant to Washington, D.C., he was twenty-six, but already world-weary.

My students come from many countries, some to get an education and return to their countries. More often, they come to escape poverty, war, and social injustice. Some suffer PTSD; other times their wounds are on the outside—a facial scar or a missing finger. Still others

157

bring their cultural biases: it isn't safe to speak openly in public, or it isn't proper to speak up in front of the opposite sex. As mentioned before in this book, such stress can interfere with their ability to express themselves or even speak. It's very troublesome when they are trying to learn a new language. My job is to create safety, while also helping them take enough risks to learn.

One day I called on Kamal to choose a quote from *The Education of a Wandering Man* by Louis L'Amour. He sat up straight and read a section with his strong French accent: "The rough times were made smoother by the realization that it was all grist for the mill, and that someday I would be writing, with knowledge, of what I was experiencing then."[1]

I met his gaze with a nod. "Nice selection. What do you think of it?"

He cleared his throat. "It's not always so easy to do what you love to do!" he said loudly. "Some people can't and some won't work at it!"

Students twisted to look, startled by his tone. His face flushed. I also blinked at his loud voice, but smiled and nodded. Like a partner in an improv skit, I was trying to listen deeply, letting him respond in safety. I moved from behind my table and podium a little closer to where he sat, still waiting.

Like a partner in an improv skit, I was learning to listen deeply.

As if he felt the attention was benevolent, Kamal continued in a quieter tone. "I don't think many people are like this author—most people don't try that hard."

"It's interesting that you say that," I said. I watched him ease back in his chair, his body softening. "Did anyone want to comment on what Kamal said?"

In this very quick moment, a shift occurred in Kamal. He participated more in his small groups over a few weeks, often volunteering to read. It was clear he now felt safe enough to learn.

When the brain feels safe, the amygdala doesn't need to fire the alarm for those stress hormones that interfere with learning. This is especially true for students under twenty-five because the neocortex, the part of the brain that develops self-control and reasoning, isn't fully developed. It is even more necessary to create safety for these students: the amygdala is fully formed but the reasoning part of the brain is not.[2]

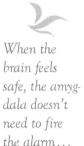

When the brain feels safe, the amygdala doesn't need to fire the alarm...

Neuroscientist David Rock credits Evian Gordon who found that the brain makes instant judgments about where a situation is safe or dangerous by tagging it. "When someone encounters a stimulus of any kind," Rock says, "their brain will either tag the stimulus as good and engage in the stimulus, or their brain will tag it as bad and disengage."[3] It makes sense. Our behavior is governed by the brain trying to minimize threat and maximize reward. When we tag a situation as a threat, the capacity to make decisions, solve problems, and interact with others decreases.[4]

When Our Brain Tags a Situation "Safe"

Anna from Poland had long hair in a ponytail and was very talkative in small group discussions. But during tests and presentations she grew very nervous, as many students did. She asked to practice with me after class, so I met with her privately to help her go over her lines of the play she was working on.

I took her script out of her hands. "Don't worry," I said. "I'll cue you if you forget. You just need to feel the emotion and motivation of your character. This will make it easier to retrieve the lines in performance."

"But...," Anna protested. "I need to look at the lines." She reached for her script, but I held on to it.

I was aware of the risk, but I also knew that safety for Anna wasn't in the memorized lines, but in trusting herself and letting her brain gain confidence. "This is about experimenting and practice. You don't need to be perfect now," I said.

In addition to her performance in a play, Anna had to give a prepared speech. She stood in front of the class, notecards in her shaking hands. Before she could begin, the class erupted in a round of applause. They had adopted this custom from the last presentation, because they were learning that each of them performed better after applause. Anna grinned and giggled back at us. Her brain had tagged the experience as safe.

"We all have those moments in life that teach us and change us," she began. "I will talk about one experience which was a turning point in my life." She barely glanced at her cards now, just spoke out, smiling.

Looking at the productivity of sixty different strategic teams, researchers found that the ideal praise to criticism ratio was 5.6 to 1. Most successful teams gave their members more than five positive remarks to every one criticism. It motivated employees to improve.[5]

Set a Boundary for Safety

But praise isn't the only requirement for safe learning. I have had to step in and set boundaries so that students feel certainty and fairness are also present. I remember one speech class where a discussion broke out about the current administration. It was election time, and opinions were strong. One man leaned forward in his chair to finally shout at another student. The other student swore back. The first student began to get out of his chair, eager for a fight.

Words came out my mouth with more calm than I felt. "It's okay to criticize people's opinions," I said firmly, "but it's not okay to criticize each other in class." The room became still. The two students sat back. The class returned to their books, unaware of the narrow bridge we had all just crossed to safety.

CHAPTER 18

Connect to the Heart

Teaching is a great way to connect with another human being, for the growth of each. My best teachers connected to both the heart and head, and gave me the most intensive learning.

The head connection is easy—we're trained how to do this early on. The heart's harder.

How can we engage the heart in our days, lives, and classroom?

For me, it means focusing on the potential of each of my students. Also, it means finding material that is uplifting, that opens us up when we study it. In other words, bigger than my own ideas. Finally, it means remembering that my job is a special opportunity to help others.

Boring material or a lack of enthusiasm for what I'm doing makes me disconnect—and it creates a classroom experience that's dull and flat.

I learned many skills in my own journey from kindergarten through grade 12. But only one subject remains with me from those early learning years. My art history teacher loved the Renaissance and Baroque painters and music. I can still hear him say the magical word *chiaroscuro* in his signature gruff voice. He also loved to say Caravaggio, pausing at the "va" sound. When he played classical music for us, his foot tapped and his head moved. My heart connected to this enthusiasm, and my body wanted to move along with the music too.

My teacher spoke as if Rembrandt, Caravaggio, and Botticelli were the most important influences on the planet. I went to the library each weekend to study these artists and their work. But it wasn't just to get a good grade; I was curious about why they were such a big deal for my teacher. I wanted to appreciate their beauty, experience such an intense love of a matter for myself.

Certain teachers in college also allowed passion for their subjects to seep into their teaching. I was depressed during my high school and college years, and it took their gentle passion to coax some excitement out of me.

A dear, short, balding theology professor woke me up from a daydream in my freshman year in college when he stood in the middle of the classroom holding *Franny and Zooey* by J.D. Salinger, reading parts of it aloud. "Do you see? Do you see?" He probed us eagerly with wild eyes. I saw a man so excited by his book and his performance that I was pulled out of my own shell. I felt like a light bulb finally getting electricity, as he nodded and directed his warm smile to me. At one point in the semester, I went to see him about my grade at midterm and we talked about the class. We were talking about questions that the characters, Franny and Zooey, had about life. He turned to me and said, "Thérèse, you seem know something about *weltschmerz.*"

When I looked up the word, I found it meant "world weary." An awareness of something grew in me. He had seen me in a way I hadn't seen myself, as all great teachers do.

164

As one of my favorite college professors said, "Real education is about those permanent things of the human spirit."[1]

There is no one secret method for good teaching. "The connections made by good teachers are held not in their methods," writes author and educator Parker J. Palmer, "but in their hearts. Meaning heart in its ancient sense, the place where intellect and emotion and spirit and will converge in the human self.... The methods used by these weavers vary widely: lectures, Socratic dialogues, laboratory experiments, collaborative problem-solving, creative chaos."[2]

If I can let myself engage with the material in a positive emotional way, I can connect with both head and heart to my students. Heart teaching requires us to stop hiding behind the mind. We have to be able to operate from that part of us that is more than thought.

To teach with heart, we have to engage our own heart intelligence.

He had seen me in a way I hadn't seen myself, as all great teachers do.

Heart Intelligence

Gabriel Gonsalves, a "heart intelligence coach" from South Africa, studied with the HeartMath Institute, a nonprofit agency that focuses on heart research. Before being able to access his own heart intelligence, Gonsalves had gone through a period of difficulty and confusion: losing his job, his mother, and his identity in a matter of weeks. It caused him to examine his life and look for a level of life that was beyond the head knowledge he had learned.

I spoke with Gonsalves by phone, wanting to know how he teaches people to access their own heart intelligence. He walked me through the process.

First, he told me, a person must acknowledge their thoughts, even welcome them. No matter what they are.

Next, he instructed me to shift from thoughts to body. Thoughts, he said, are normally about the future or the past. "But when we are in the body, we are in the present moment. This is where breath, voice, and senses are," he added.

It sounded a lot like focusing (see chapter 14), but directed to the heart.

"But when we are in the body, we are in the present moment."[3]

"Now shift away from body," he said. "There's an energy in the body beyond the senses that is moving. There's a quality in the heart or stomach that is deeper than the senses. You can call that angry, sad, hopeful, stressed, whatever. Or give it a color or a temperature to get rid of labels. When we can connect more to the quality of the energy beyond the label, we can dip into the energy behind the emotions." As he spoke, I tried each step, letting myself experience the expansion.

He put in a cautionary note. "If you shift directly from the mind to the heart, it's the mind imitating the heart and not the true heart intelligence."

When only mind is running the show, the system can get stressed because it can produce fear. "When your heart is running the show, it will harmonize the body," he assured me.[3]

There was a good chance to practice this soon after, when I gave a talk on tools for self-improvement. Two friends were helping me on this Saturday afternoon in spring. The sun outside was high and bright in the Florida sky as we talked about our teaching techniques that would help attendees with goals, relationships, and everyday problems.

My friends and I arrived early and set up the room. One of my friends handed out pen and paper to guests. About fifteen came.

For this workshop, we prepared as we would for any class with a set curriculum, but this workshop topic was more personal for me. I knew it would require more than trust in my head; I'd have to rely on heart intelligence to listen to these truth seekers. We were talking about real life here, with all its challenges. At one point during our presentation, a heavy-set man spoke up. His face looked strained, from worry or pain, and he sat with his hands folded. His words came out slowly. "I lost my son a year ago in an accident," he said, "and I haven't gotten over it." He paused, resettling in his chair. "I still don't understand why it happened."

The room went silent. Everyone looked at me. My partner was behind me, quietly shuffling his notes. What are you possibly going to say to this?! I thought, beginning to panic. Whatever you say will diminish his pain!

Remembering Gonsalves's advice, I dropped my attention away from my head and into my heart. I put my attention on sensing my heart intelligence, tuning in to its steady beat. Slowly I felt a softness and heat in my chest. I allowed this soft feeling to grow, like I was leaving the language center of my brain and falling into the truer energy living in my heart.

All eyes were still on me. I felt two tears slide down my face. I wiped them away. Simple words came out. "I am so sorry for your loss." I didn't pretend or act, I didn't try to fix him or control the outcome—and I didn't know what would happen.

The man exhaled and relaxed back into his chair. My friend who still sat at the door sent me a smile and a nod. Compassion was all that was needed in that moment. But I had to travel from my mind to my heart to experience it. It was different from pity or sympathy. I was connecting to this man at the heart level. My colleague and I finished our talk and the man stayed behind and talked to me about his son. Two other people spoke with him about coping strategies they had used for grief, as they too had suffered losses not long ago. As the man left, he still had pain in his eyes, but something in him had relaxed.

Practice from the Heart

It takes time to learn and trust these ways of teaching. We're not trained in this method of connecting with our students. But over time, we learn. As a teacher, you can't call in sick or let someone else take over your class, so initial terror gradually subsides as you keep facing the students, keep teaching through the fear, using these new tools to move past it.

In the early years especially, if a student acted up, I got defensive. Hesitant in my words and actions, I stopped taking risks. I let less of my heart come forward. Of course, over time, this choice made things worse for everyone. The class became dull. I still followed the curriculum, I taught the subject matter, but the students didn't enjoy learning, because not as much of me was present in class.

New Research on the Coherent Heart

Scientists from the HeartMath Institute have discovered patterns of coherence and incoherence in the heart by measuring the pattern of wave intervals using an electrocardiogram monitor. They call this means of measuring coherence in the heart the Heart Rate Variability pattern (HRV).[4]

When the HRV pattern is incoherent, the subject is in a negative emotional state, like anger or frustration. Incoherent patterns influence the brain's ability to remember and function. A coherent HRV pattern comes about when a person is in a positive emotional state, like gratitude or play, love or appreciation.[5] In this coherent state, the thinking brain can "optimally receive and create patterns from incoming information," according to researchers.[6]

It's a no-brainer: If we are in a positive heart state, we can learn better. But not only that. If we are coherent, or positive, we can also affect those around us.

If a student is incoherent—angry, inattentive, uncooperative—that incoherence affects the other students and it affects me. The classroom synergy drops.

HeartMath Institute has also found that when one person's heart becomes coherent, it affects everyone within a six-foot radius. This is because the heart is electrical. It produces the largest amount of electrical energy in our bodies, about forty to sixty times more than the brain.[7] We are very influential beings, in many ways.

Carla Hannaford and quantum physicists agree. "We are vibrational interference patterns rather than matter. We live in a sea of vibration," says Hannaford. "Within the unified field, these vibrations affect us from our environment.... Within this field we're all connected."[8]

The journey to harmony is filled with trials, but also many rewards. To live with the open heart, using our heart intelligence, is the hero's journey that Joseph Campbell and others wrote about. It calls on us to face our fears, to take action, to make mistakes, to bring more of ourselves to the classroom. Like Orpheus who had to make his journey into hell to come back to earth with greater awareness and love, we sometimes have to journey into difficult situations to learn how to become more resourceful as teachers—using the knowledge within our heads but sensing more with our hearts.

My journey in life, in the stories I've told throughout this book, have been about how I learned to live openly, in the moment, with the resources of the head and the heart. And about how this made me a better teacher. As it can you.

Afterword: Performing Poetry

Last July, I read my original poetry in front of about two hundred people. It was a very nerve-wracking experience. I rehearsed beforehand in a small hotel room off to the side of the large performance hall. The flute player who performed with me was a tall man who had a lot of experience. As we stood in the tiny rehearsal room, our backs to the window which overlooked a courtyard, I spoke my poems, but my voice came out flat and forced.

After five run-throughs, the flute player and I were mechanically in sync, but there was little spark running through me or out into the room. We left the room to wait backstage, my heart far away.

I heard the emcee say our names. We walked to the center of the stage. I was suddenly aware of the audience and the physical space of the stage, my feet on the floor, and the air as it touched my arms. I looked out and felt the energy of the audience. An electrical thrill went through me, and I could feel my heart open wider. I had to fight back tears, as the emotion and heart expansion passed through my scared body.

The flute player gave me the cue and I launched into the first poem. Each consonant, each vowel now had resonance. Each moment, witnessed by the audience, carried more significance. The reading and flute playing was about everyone in the room. We all created a performance together that was the magnetic power of everyone.

171

As I finished and looked out at the crowd, I saw my friends and family members in the third row, smiling wide. A surge of joy ran through me.

I thought of Zarmina and her song. I thought of the freedom and egoless performance that she had shown us all those years ago as she sang her final presentation. She had tapped into something universal, as I had on that stage. The thing that moved us, that transformed us all to tears, is what can happen in authentic teaching and learning. There was no pride or fear for Zarmina as she connected to us through her heart. As I had felt just then, too.

The danger in higher education is too much thinking—or too much of one type of thinking. Sounds like a contradiction, I know. We have to engage more of our students' brains, yes, but also their bodies, emotions, and hearts. This is what Zarmina shared with us that one spring day in class. This is what I wanted to share with you in these pages.

Free from fear, there is a give and take between audience and actors, students and teachers. The harmony of heart and head and body can become a channel for something greater than any of us can imagine.

Endnotes

Introduction: Zarmina's Story

1. Yo-Yo Ma, interviewed by Charlie Rose, *The Charlie Rose Show*, PBS, October 16, 2013, *http://charlierose.com/watch/60284600*.

Chapter 1: My Story

1. Frank Herbert, *Dune* (New York: Penguin, 1965), 8.
2. Hannah Devlin, "What Is Functional Magnetic Resonance Imaging?," accessed November 28, 2015, PsychCentral.com, *http://psychcentral.com/lib/what-is-functional-magnetic-resonance-imaging-fmri/*.
3. Robert Sapolsky, YouTube video, accessed May 2014, *http://www.youtube.com/watch?v=8ysG9ay8TAs*. This video is no longer accessible, but here is a current source of his work: *http://greatergood.berkeley.edu/article/item/how_to_relieve_stress*.
4. Sharon Begley, "The Brain: How the Brain Rewires Itself," *TIME*, January 19, 2007, *http://content.time.com/time/magazine/article/0,9171,1580438,00.html*.

Chapter 2: Free Your Voice

1. Mary Lowenthal Felstiner, "Alfred Wolfsohn," *Voice Movement Therapy.com*, accessed September 18, 2015, *http://www.vmtuk.com/Alfred_Wolfsohn.html*.
2. Sheila Braggins, "The Way Alfred Wolfsohn Taught," transcript of lecture given at Myths of the Voice Festival, Pan Summer University, Roy Hart Theatre archive, Malerargues, France, July 2005. *http://roy-hart.com/sheila2.htm*.
3. Sheila Braggins, "Alfred Wolfsohn, the Man and His Ideas," Roy Hart Theatre archive, Malerargues, France, *http://www.roy-hart.com/sheila.htm*.

4. Kristin Linklater, *Freeing the Natural Voice* (New York: Drama Book Publishers 1976), 73.

5. Catherine Fitzmaurice, interviewed by Saul Kotzubei, 2005. VoiceCoachLA.com, accessed November 28, 2015, *http://static1.squarespace.com/static/52913f20e4b09bd01793 d4ba/t/52a00e5ce4b0bdf80ef84865/1386221148456 /Interview+of+Catherine+Fitzmaurice.pdf.*

6. Braggins, "The Way Alfred Wolfsohn Taught."

7. Smithsonian Folkways. Accessed Feb. 1, 2016 *http://www. folkways.si.edu/vox-humana-alfred-wolfsohns-experiments-in -extension-of-human-vocal-range/contemporary-electronic-science -nature-sounds/album/smithsonian*

   In "Vox Humana: Alfred Wolfsohn's Experiments in Extension of Human Vocal Range," there are recordings of some of Wolfsohn's students, done around 1956. Students recorded themselves singing in duets accompanying by violin, viola, and cello.

   "Duet in New Vocal Sound Range," the second sound file on the web page for Folkways Records, is an example of a female voice starting high and ending in the bass register, and a male voice starting in the bass range and ending in a high ultra-soprano range.

Chapter 3: Follow Your Passion or . . .

1. Julian Ford and Jon Wortmann, *Hijacked by Your Brain* (Naperville, IL: Sourcebooks, 2013), 29–30.

2. Ibid., 25.

3. Ibid., 12.

4. Ibid., 146.

Chapter 4: Break Free with Movement

1. Carla Hannaford, *SmartMoves: Why Learning Is Not All in Your Head* (Salt Lake City: Great River Books [formerly Great Ocean Publishers], 1995), 235.

2. Andrea Isaacs, Enneamotion.com, accessed January 1, 2015, *http://www.enneamotion.com/Emotional-Literacy-Articles /Emotional-Literacy-Articles.html.*

3. Ibid.

4. Hannaford, *SmartMoves*, 195.

5. Ibid., 196.

6. Alex Korb, "Yoga: Changing the Brain's Stressful Habits," *Prefrontal Nudity* (blog) on *Psychology Today*, September 7, 2011, *https://cdn.psychologytoday.com/blog/prefrontal-nudity/201109/yoga-changing-the-brains-stressful-habits*.

7. Carla Hannaford, interview by the author, Summer 2013.

8. Hannaford, *SmartMoves*, 125.

9. Donna Eden and David Feinstein, *Energy Medicine for Women* (New York: Tarcher/Penguin, 2008), 62–63.

Chapter 5: The Rhythm and Magic of Shakespeare

1. "Inner-City Teacher Takes No Shortcuts to Success," narrated by Michelle Trudeau. NPR, April 26, 2005, *www.npr.org/books/authors/138334125/rafe-esquith*.

2. Rafe Esquith, *Real Talk for Real Teachers* (New York: Viking, 2013), 309.

3. Ibid., 312.

4. Ben Crystal, interviewed by Lee Jamieson, "Performing Shakespeare," About.com Education, accessed November 28, 2015, *http://shakespeare.about.com/od/interviews/a/performing_shax.htm*.

5. Ken Ludwig, *How Shakespeare Can Make You a Better Actor*, published on *backstage.com*. Also available at *http://www.kenludwig.com/articles/how_shakespeare_can_make_your_child_a_better_actor.php* accessed November 30, 2015.

6. Michael York, interviewed by Andrea Grossman, WritersBloc at the Writer's Guild Theatre, Los Angeles, April 16, 2001, accessed September 13, 2015, *http://www.writersblocpresents.com/archives/shakespeare/shakespeare.htm*.

7. Ken Ludwig, lecture presented at Politics and Prose Bookstore, Washington, D.C., July 24, 2013, *http://www.youtube.com/watch?v=8ZPmMwP7bzY*.

Chapter 6: Using Props, Costumes, and Sound for Transformation

1. Charles Moore, interviewed by Toby Harnden, *After Words*, C-SPAN2 Book TV, May 22, 2013, *http://www.c-span.org /video/?312769-1/words-charles-moore*.
2. Brian Bates, *The Way of the Actor* (Boston: Shambhala Publications, 1987), 30–31.
3. Meryl Streep, interviewed by Terry Gross, *FreshAir*, NPR, February 7, 2012, *http://www.npr.org/2012/02/06/146362798 /meryl-streep-the-fresh-air-interview*.
4. Meryl Streep, interviewed by Holly Williams, *ContactMusic .com*, December 25, 2014, *http://www.contactmusic.com /meryl-streep/news/meryl-streep-into-the-woods-costume_4516433*.
5. Bates, *Way of the Actor*, chapter 6.

Chapter 7: Imaginative Techniques

1. Amy Cuddy, "Your Body Language Shapes Who You Are," video lecture at TED Talks, June 2012, *https://www.ted.com /talks/amy_cuddy_your_body_language_shapes_who_you_are ?language=en*.
2. Ibid.
3. John Corcoran Foundation, "John's Story," accessed September 13, 2015, *http://www.johncorcoranfoundation.org/about /corcoran/*.

Chapter 8: The Horse Whisperer

1. Julie Goldman, director, *Buck*, IFC Films, 2011.
2. Kenneth Wesson, "Learning and Memory: How Do We Remember and Why Do We Often Forget?," *Brain World Magazine.com*, March 1, 2012, *http://brainworldmagazine.com /learning-memory-how-do-we-remember-and-why-do-we-often-forget/*.

Chapter 9: Traumas and Learning: What do Solders and Scientists Say about Anxiety and PTSD?

1. Bryan Brown, in discussion with the author, November, 2013.

2. Matthew Tull, "Traumatic Exposure and PTSD in College Students," About Health.com, accessed November 28, 2015, *http://ptsd.about.com/od/prevalence/a/PTSDinCollegeStudents .htm*.

3. Kristin Towhill, in discussion with the author, April, 2014.

Chapter 10: Just Breathe

1. Carla Hannaford, *Playing in the Unified Field: Raising and Becoming Conscious, Creative Human Beings*, (Salt Lake City: Great River Books, 2010) 27.

2. Peter C. Brown, Henry L. Roediger III, Mark A. McDaniel, *Make it Stick* (Cambridge: Harvard University Press, 2014)

3. John Lupos, "The Importance to Your Health of Deep Abdominal Breathing," YMAA.com, April 12, 2010, *http:// ymaa.com/articles/the-importance-to-your-heath-of-deep-adbominal -breathing*.

4. Robert Sapolsky, "The Documentary," and "Q&A: Why does psychological stress turn on the stress response? From *Stress: Portrait of a Killer"* National Geographic and Robert Sapolsky. Accessed November, 2015, *http://killerstress.stanford .edu/more/*.

5. Chunyi Lin, "Breathing of the Universe," Spring Forest Qigong, accessed November 28, 2015, *http://www .springforestqigong.com/breathing-of-the-univer*se.

Chapter 11: Slow Down

1. Ford and Wortmann, *Hijacked by Your Brain*, 69.

2. Robert Bjork, "Desirable Difficulties: Slowing Down Learn-ing," video lecture, Go Cognitive.net, accessed September 14, 2015, *http://gocognitive.net/interviews/desirable-difficulties -slowing-down-learning*.

3. Robert J. Stahl, "Using 'Think-Time' and 'Wait-Time' Skill-fully in the Classroom," ERIC Digest.org, May 1994, *http:// www.ericdigests.org/1995-1/think.htm*.

4. Nicolas Carr, *In the Shallows: What the Internet Is Doing to Our Brains* (New York: W.W. Norton, 2010), 221.

5. Chunyi Lin, "Breathing of the Universe" Youtube video, May 5, 2009, *https://www.youtube.com/watch?v=nXwIRRTv7z4.*

Chapter 12: Pay Attention!

1. AZ *Quotes*, Robert Redford as quoted on web page. Accessed February 10, 2016. *www.azquotes.com/quote/569229.*

2. Carr. *In the Shallows*, 194.

3. Sir Kenneth Robinson, "Changing Paradigms," lecture for Royal Society for the Encouragement of Arts, Manufactures and Commerce, June 16, 2008, *https://www.thersa.org /discover/videos/event-videos/2008/06/changing-paradigms/.*

4. Developmental Cognitive Neuroscience Lab of Adele Diamond, University of British Columbia, *devcogneuro.com/index .html.* Adele Diamond's program "Tools of the Mind" uses drama and other tools to help children learn to regulate their attention and behavior.

5. Helga Noice and Tony Noice, "What Studies of Actors and Acting Can Tell Us About Memory and Cognitive Functioning," *Current Directions in Psychological Science* 15, no.1 (2006), 14-18, *http://www.psychologicalscience.org/pdf/cd/actors _memory.pdf.*

6. Line Goguen-Hughes, "Lights, Camera, Meditation," Mindful.org, January 17, 2011, *http://www.mindful.org/in-your-life /arts-and-creativity/lights-camera-meditation.*

7. Ellen Langer, quoted in Winifred Gallagher, *Rapt: Attention and the Focused Life* (New York, Penguin, 2009), 137–38.

8. Ellen Langer, *The Power of Mindful Learning* (Cambridge, MA: Perseus Books, 1997), 39.

9. Ibid., 43.

10. Jill Suttie, "Mindful Kids, Peaceful Schools," Greater Good, June 1, 2007, *http://greatergood.berkeley.edu/article/item /mindful_kids_peaceful_schools.*

11. Ibid.

12. Susan Kaiser Greenland, "Author Susan Kaiser Greenland offers tips on how to help your kids manage stress," YouTube video, March 11, 2010, *https://www.youtube.com /watch?v=D9GJtic9eW0.*

13. Wendy Hasenkamp and Lawrence Barsalon in Daniel Gold-man, "Exercising the Mind to Treat Attention Deficits," *Well* (blog), *New York Times*, May 12, 2014, *http://well.blogs.nytimes. com/2014/05/12/exercising-the-mind-to-treat -attention-deficits/?_r=0.*

Chapter 13: Survive and Thrive with the Growth Mindset

1. Shunryu Suzuki, *Zen Mind, Beginner's Mind* (Boston: Sham-bhala Publications, 2006), 21.

2. Stephen Nachmonovitch, *Free Play: Improvisation in Life and Art* (New York: Tarcher/Putnam, 1991), 68.

3. Carol Dweck, Mindsetonline.com, accessed November 30, 2015, *http://mindsetonline.com/whatisit/about/.*

4. Ibid., Mindset Online.com.

5. Rafe Esquith, *Real Talk for Real Teachers* (New York: Viking, 2013), 10–15.

6. Ibid., 14.

7. Angela Duckworth, "The Key to Success? Grit," video lecture at TED talks, April 2013, *http://www.ted.com/talks/angela _lee_duckworth_the_key_to_success_grit?language=en.*

8. Carol Dweck, *Mindset: The New Psychology of Success* (New York: Random House, 2006), 8–18.

9. Carol Dweck, interviewed by Gary Hopkins, "How Can Teachers Develop Students' Motivation and Success?," *Education World*, February 7, 2000. *http://www.educationworld .com/a_issues/chat/chat010.shtml.*

10. Malcolm Gladwell, *Outliers*, (New York: Little Brown and Co., 2008).

11. Susan Jeffers, *Embracing Uncertainty: Breakthrough Methods for Achieving Peace of Mind When Facing the Unknown* (New York: St. Martin's Press, 2003), 32.

12. Konstantin Novoselov, interviewed by Gary Taubes, Science-Watch.com, February 2009, *http://archive.sciencewatch.com /ana/st/graphene/09febSTGraNovo/.*

13. Ibid.

Chapter 14: It Takes Guts

1. Jalal al-Din Rumi, "The Guest House," in *The Essential Rumi*, translated by Coleman Barks with John Moyne (New York: Harper Collins, 1995), 109. Reprinted by permission of Coleman Barks.

2. Eugene T. Gendlin, *Focusing* Available online at the Focusing Institute, *http://www.focusing.org/gendlin/docs/gol_2234.html*. Used by permission.

3. Ann Weiser Cornell, *The Power of Focusing: A Practical Guide to Emotional Self-Healing* (New York: MJF Books, 1996), 8.

4. Gendlin, *Focusing*, online version.

5. Michael Gershon, *The Second Brain*, (New York: Harper Collins Publishers, 1998).

6. Patricia Omidian and Nina Joy Lawrence, "A Community-Based Approach to Focusing: The Islam and Focusing Project of Afghanistan," *The Folio*, 2007, 156, accessed November 28, 2015, *https://focusing.org/folio/Vol20No12007/17 _CommunityBased.pdf*.

7. Sue Grenham, Gerard Clarke, John F. Cryan, and Timothy G. Dinan, "Brain-Gut-Microbe Communication in Health and Disease," *Frontiers in Physiology*, vol. 2, 94 (December 7, 2011), *http://www.ncbi.nlm.nih.gov/pmc/articles /PMC3232439/*.

Chapter 15: Peaceful Warrior Teacher

1. Dan Millman, *The Way of the Peaceful Warrior* (Tiburon, CA: H.J. Kramer/New World Library, 2000), 209. Used by permission

2. See more on EFT and Gary Craig at *http://emofree.com/*. Used by permission.

3. Brad Yates, telephone conversation with the author, March, 2010.

4. Millman, *Peaceful Warrior*, 152. Used by permission.

Chapter 16: Say Yes to Improv(e) Your Life

1. Tina Fey, interviewed by Brian Williams, *Nightly News*, NBC, December 28, 2009, *http://www.nbcnews.com/video/nightly -news/34586457#34586457*.

2. Tina Fey, interviewed by James Lipton, BravoTV, March 14, 2013, *https://www.youtube.com/watch?v=BSffouc4i98*.

3. Keith Johnstone, *Impro: Improvisation and the Theatre* (New York: Routledge Press, 2015), 96. Used by permission.

4. Ibid., 96. Used by permission.

5. Charles Limb, "What Does a Creative Brain Look Like?," TED talk, NPR, May 6, 2015, *http://www.npr.org/2014/10/03/351549673/what-does-a-creative-brain-look-like*.

6. Bob Stanek and Charna Halpern, inteviewed by Jacki Lyden, "Can Physicists Be Funny?" NPR, September 6, 2008, *http://www.npr.org/templates/story/story.php?storyId=94357426*.

Chapter 17: The "Safe" Approach to Learning Language

1. Louis L'Amour, The Education of a Wandering Man (New York: Bantam Books, 1990), 148.

2. Richard Friedman, "Why Teenagers Act Crazy," New York Times, June 28, 2014, http://psleaders.com/publicsafetyleadership/tag/neuroscience-and-crime/.

3. David Rock, "SCARF: A Brain-based Model for Collaborating with and Influencing Others," Neuroleadership Journal, vol. 1, no. 1 (2008), http://www.strategicplay.ca/upload/documents/nlj_scarfus.pdf.

4. Ibid.

5. Jack Zenger and Joseph Folkman, "The Ideal Praise-to-Criticism Ratio," Harvard Business Review, March 15, 2013, https://hbr.org/2013/03/the-ideal-praise-to-criticism.

Chapter 18: Connect to the Heart

1. James V. Schall, "The Final Gladness," lecture at the Tocqueville Forum, Berkley Center, Georgetown University, Washington, D.C., December 14, 2012, https://www.youtube.com/watch?v=xN1rFyYbKak.

2. Parker Palmer, "The Heart of a Teacher," Center for Courage and Renewal.org, November 1997, http://www.couragerenewal.org/parker/writings/heart-of-a-teacher/.

3. Gabriel Gonsalves, interviewed by author, July 9, 2014.

4. HeartMath Institute, "Personality and Heart Rate Variability: Exploring Pathways from Personality to Cardiac Coherence and Health," November, 2013, *https://www.heartmath.org/*.

5. Carla Hannaford, *Playing in the Unified Field* (Salt Lake City, UT: Great River Books, 2010), 61.

6. Victoria Tennant, "The Powerful Impact of Stress," Johns Hopkins School of Education.edu, September 2005, *http:// education.jhu.edu/PD/newhorizons/strategies/topics /Keeping%20Fit%20for%20Learning/stress.html*. Author cites Childre and Martin, *The HeartMath Solution* (New York, HarperCollins, 1999), 37.

7. HeartMath Institute, "The Energetic Heart Is Unfolding," July 22, 2010, *http://www.heartmath.org/free-services/articles -of-the-heart/energetic-heart-is-unfolding.html*.

8. Hannaford, *Unified Field*, chapter 4.

Acknowledgments

There are many people to thank for helping me get this book from idea to finish.

Thank you to my students over the years who have helped me learn the art of teaching. This book is in part because of and for them. Thank you to my early teaching mentors at Northern Virginia Community College, especially Dr. Elizabeth Hammer, Mariette Johnson, Brenda Conerly, Gillie Campbell, Kathy Wax and Nancy Hoagland. During my early years, they were there with open and patient hearts to encourage me when I needed it most. Thanks to the administrators at Northern Virginia Community College, who saw the benefits of drama and movement in learning and showed their support through a sabbatical.

Thank you to Mary Carroll Moore whose classes and coaching helped me not give up, helped me learn the rigor of writing, and to appreciate the importance of peer review and editing. This book could not have materialized without her teaching and editing. Thank you, too, to my classmates in those online classes, especially Sara, Katherine, Danielle, and Clare who went through my chapters with care and keen eyes.

Thanks to the generous people who allowed me to speak to them and share some of their stories, especially Bryan Brown, Kristin (Kiki) Towhill, Gabriel Gonsalves, Carla Hannaford, and Parker Palmer. They walk the talk of what they do. Many thanks to Al Harris, whom I found when I was ready to go no further, and who listened with a careful ear to help me take my book to the next step: a true synthesizer of material.

Thank you to Coleman Barks for giving me permission to use his translation of the Rumi poem. Thanks to the Focusing Institute, Dan Millman, and Gary Craig for permission to reprint their work.

Many thanks to to Robin Adams McBride for her creative layout and cover design. It was a pleasure!

Thanks to those dynamic healers along the way, especially Jen Ward.

Thank you to my father, James Aylward, for his love and support. I'm grateful to my mother for propelling me on this journey. Much gratitude to my niece, Caroline, for her interview and to my aunt, Helen Mulligan, for her love and support.

And finally, thanks to those who embrace a different way of learning and expressing their creativity in the world. And to those who have to relearn how to use their voice after a period of stress and isolation or in order to adapt to a new culture. I hope this book helps you.

About the Author

Thérèse Ayla Kravetz is a writer, teacher, and speaker. After years as an actor and voice coach, she taught English at a community college in Virginia to international students. She discovered out of necessity how to "re-wire" her anxious brain and to help her students do the same by using voice, movement, breathing, drama and more. She noticed these tools accelerated learning for her students as they bypassed anxiety to be creative and confident in the present moment. Her books, her blog, and her teaching show others how to transform the fight or flight response and tune into their own authentic voice and creativity. She won a sabbatical to pursue her work in this field. She has an M.Ed. from Lesley University, and a B.S. from Georgetown. She lives in Florida with her husband, Mike, and her very special dogs, and cat.

54458223R00110

Made in the USA
Charleston, SC
05 April 2016